Beginner's Guide to Using Sewing Patterns

Beginner's Guide to Using Sewing Patterns

Kathleen Blaxland

Kangaroo Press

To my husband,
who gave me continual encouragement,
my mother and father,
and my daughters, Jennifer and Susan,
with love

© Kathleen Blaxland 1993

*First published in 1993 by Kangaroo Press Pty Ltd
3 Whitehall Road Kenthurst NSW 2156 Australia
P.O. Box 6125 Dural Delivery Centre NSW 2158
Typeset by G.T. Setters Pty Limited
Printed in Singapore through Global Com Pte Ltd*

ISBN 0 86417 534 5

Contents

Introduction 7
Sewing kit 8
Sewing with a sewing machine 8
Sewing samples 9
Pressing 9
Body measurement charts 10
   Girls 10
   Boys 11
   Taking measurements 10
Needle and thread chart 12
Reading a pattern 13
The toile 15
Cutting out 16
Tacking 16
Basting 17
Tailor tacks 17
Seams 18
   Stitched and turned seam 18
   Zigzagged seam 18
   Hand-sewn overcast seam 18
   French seam 19
   Run and fell seam 19
   Hong Kong seam 19
Facings 20
Interfacing 21
Understitching 21
Topstitching 22
Darts 24
   Bodice darts 24
   French darts 24
   Contour darts 25

Bias strips 26
Bindings 27
Rouleaus 28
Gathering 29
Collars 30
   Pointed collar 30
   Peter Pan collar 30
   Shirt collar 31
Cuffs 32
Waistband 41
Setting in a zip 42
Sleeves 45
   Set-in sleeve 45
   Shirt sleeve 46
   Raglan sleeve 46
Pockets 48
Pleats 50
Hand-sewing 51
Buttonholes 52
Sewing on buttons 53
   Sew-through buttons 53
   Shank buttons 53
Hooks and eyes 54
Patterns
   Gathered skirt with Liberty print border and sash 56
   Pleated skirt 59
   Pinafore 62
   Party frock 65
   Board shorts 68
Index 70

Introduction

This book is a guide to help young beginners learn to sew and to understand commercial sewing patterns. If the samples are sewn in the order they are presented in the book, and practised until they are fully understood, by the time you have worked through the book you should be able to make the garments shown in the photographs on pages 37–40. The instructions are straightforward, with easy instructions on how to draft the patterns given on pages 56–69.

The garments you can make include a pleated skirt, a gathered skirt with a cottage print border and sash, a stretch knit striped pinafore, a fun party frock with frothy frills, and easy-to-sew board shorts.

It is an art to take a flat piece of material and make it into a convex shape to fit the body. Sewing can be a wonderful hobby, and relieve the boredom of rainy holidays. You can set up the family sewing machine, pick a simple pattern and a happy print and have the satisfaction of making yourself a fun garment. You will also save lots of money. You can even buy your own labels to give your clothes that professional finish.

It might be that after a bit of practice, and some success with your own clothes, you could start taking orders from friends. A few sales at a small profit would soon add up to quite a bit of pocketmoney. Many famous couturiers have started out this way.

Good luck with your early sewing days!

Sewing kit

1. Sharp dressmaking scissors, to be used *only* on fabric, *never* on anything else.
2. Cheaper scissors for cutting patterns.
3. A tin of dressmaker's pins.
4. Tape measure.
5. Tailor's chalk to mark fabric.
6. Unpicker.
7. A packet of sewing needles in graded sizes.
8. A selection of cotton and polyester sewing threads. You must select the correct thread for a fabric to avoid tensioning problems with the sewing machine. The Needle and Thread Chart on page 12 is very helpful here.
9. Cheaper cottons can be used for tacking, provided they are the same colour as your garment.
10. Sewing basket to hold everything.
11. One metre of plain-coloured lawn to sew your samples.
12. Folder with clear plastic pages to hold your samples.
13. Small (12 cm) zip to sew your zip sample.
14. Thimble.

Sewing with a sewing machine

1. Have a clean neat area to work in.
2. Check that the sewing machine is in good working order.
3. Put in a new sewing machine needle for each garment you sew, the correct size for the fabric you are using (see Needle and Thread Chart on page 12).
4. Use the correct thread for the fabric you are working with or the stitch will gather the fabric. Remember that thread sews in a shade lighter than it appears on the reel, so choose colours carefully.
5. Make sure your scissors are sharp and only used for cutting material.
6. Have your pin tin handy; as you remove pins from the garment, place them in the tin.
7. Have the ironing board set up and test the fabric for the correct temperature. Always keep a press-cloth handy for fabrics which can't take direct heat.
8. It takes practice to sew in a straight line. For practice, draw straight lines with a biro on some scrap fabric. Keep your eye on the needle and on the lines. Hold the material front and back to help guide the stitching. Try not to go too fast—a steady even pace will give you the best results.

Sewing samples

Once you have mastered sewing straight lines with a sewing machine, it is very important to practise sewing samples. This will give you an awareness of the techniques and skills required before you begin to sew a garment.

Keep your samples in a folder with clear plastic pages. Give each one a heading. You will find them a very helpful reference, the beginnings of the practical skills of sewing, and a way of learning the theory.

Remember, practice makes perfect.

Your sample folder should contain:
Stitched and turned seam
French seam
Run and fell seam
Neck facing
Binding a neckline
Making a rouleau
Darts
Waistband
Setting a zip
Slipstitching
Hand-sewn buttonholes
Machine-sewn buttonholes
Sewing on buttons

1. Make small scale paper patterns of each sample first (15 cm is a good length for seam samples).
2. You will need a 12 cm zip for the zip sample.
3. A contrasting coloured fabric for the neck facing and binding a neckline samples will help distinguish the parts. The plain coloured lawn fabric always represents the actual garment (see the photograph on page 34).
4. The waistband sample is cut to an 18 cm length (page 41).
5. Iron the lawn before cutting out samples.
6. Keep making samples until you fully understand all the instructions. Keep the best ones for your sample book.
7. Decorate your sample book with cut-out pictures of garments from famous couturiers, or the couturiers themselves—a visual suggestion of a future career.

Pressing

Pressing your garment step-by-step as you sew will give professional results.

There is a difference between pressing and ironing:

Pressing is the process of lifting and lowering the iron. The combination of heat, weight and steam allows you to shape the garment as you sew.

Ironing is when the iron is pushed over the material with a rotating movement, e.g. ironing a tablecloth or something flat.

1. Never press over pins, because they will leave marks in your fabric.
2. A covered shoulder pad is useful to hold under the garment in difficult curved or gathered areas.
3. Keep a press-cloth handy for fabrics that cannot take a direct iron, e.g. wool, velvet and some fine silks.
4. Before starting work on a new garment, test a sample piece of fabric to find the correct temperature.
5. A garment made in a heavier fabric, e.g. wool or taffeta, which you have pressed through each stage, will benefit from being professionally pressed at the drycleaners when it is finished. Label it clearly with a stitched-on label which says: 'New Garment, Press Only, Please'.

Body measurement charts

Girls

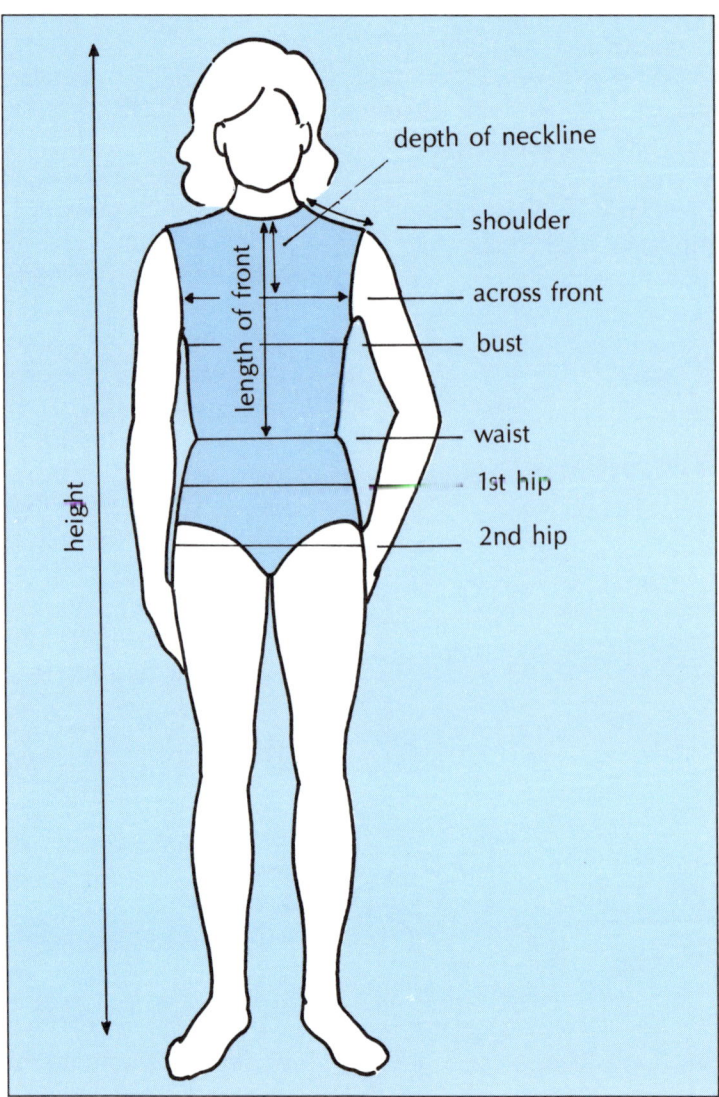

Taking measurements

Ask someone else to take your measurements so they will be accurate. It's almost impossible to measure yourself.

Waist Tie a cord around the waist to find its exact position. If making a skirt to be worn with a blouse tucked in, allow extra on this measurement for comfort.

Bust Around the fullest part of the bust.
Length front Measure from the highest point of the shoulder over the bust and down to the waist.
Length back From centre back neck down to waist.
Across front Measure from armhole to armhole at the highest point of the bust.
Across back Measure from armhole to

Boys

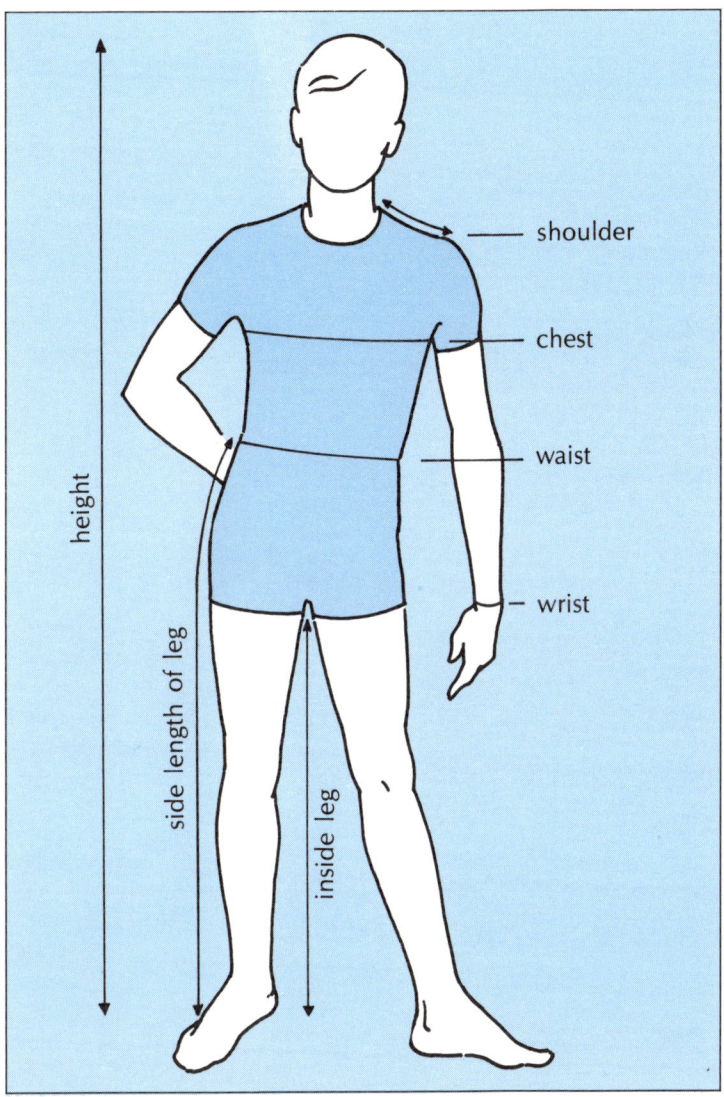

armhole one-quarter of the way down from the nape of neck to the waistline.

1st hip area Measure around the hip 10 cm below the waistline.

2nd hip area Measure around largest part of the hip, usually 20.5 cm below first hip measurement.

Shoulder Taken from neck edge to shoulder bone.

Length of arm Bend elbow, run tape from shoulder edge around elbow and down to wrist.

Waist to crotch Sit on a flat chair with back straight. Measure from waist to seat; allow 3–4 cm for comfort.

Side length of leg From waist to floor; allow for hem and seams.

Inside leg From crotch to floor; allow for hem and seams.

Needle and thread chart

Fabric weight	Threads	Machine needle size
Very Light: Georgette, organza, lingerie fabrics, heirloom sewing	Cotton-covered polyester— extra fine	60–70
Light: Handkerchief linen, lawn, paper taffeta, lace	Cotton-covered polyester	70
Medium Light: Gingham, satin, sheeting	Cotton-covered polyester	70–80
Medium: Flannel, corduroy, linen, velvet, poplin, shantung	Cotton-covered polyester	70–90
Medium heavy: Denim, garbardine, felt, textured linen	100% polyester	90–100
Heavy: Corduroy, sailcloth, ticking	100% polyester heavy duty	100–110
Very heavy: Canvas, upholstery fabrics	100% polyester heavy duty	110
Leathers and vinyls: Leather, suedes, chamois	Spun polyester	90–100 Leather wedge point
Stretch materials: Knits, stretch velours	100% polyester	70–80 Ballpoint

Reading a pattern

Commercially produced sewing patterns have a picture of the garment printed on the front of the packet and on the back a description of the garment's sewing structure (or construction). If the pattern includes more than one garment, or more than one variation of the same garment, they are usually distinguished by labels such as A, B, C.

Size

Size is important. Make sure the pattern you choose is as close to your measurements as possible. Take time to study the pattern before you begin cutting out.

Cutting layout

The cutting layout shows the position of pattern pieces on the fabric; position will depend on your size and on the width of the material.

Selvedge

The selvedge of a fabric is the firmly woven edge on each side of a length of fabric. It is made during the weaving process on the loom. Remove selvedges when cutting out a garment to prevent puckering in the seamline.

Direction arrows

Fabric can run three ways in a garment. The pattern pieces carry long arrows which show you the way your material should be cut:
Lengthwise arrows are used where the grainline of the fabric runs parallel with the selvedge in the pattern piece. The thread in this direction is called the *warp*.
Arrows across the grainline (horizontal to the selvedge) indicate that the pattern piece follows the crosswise thread called the *weft*.
Diagonal (bias) arrows are used where the material is folded into a triangle on a 45°

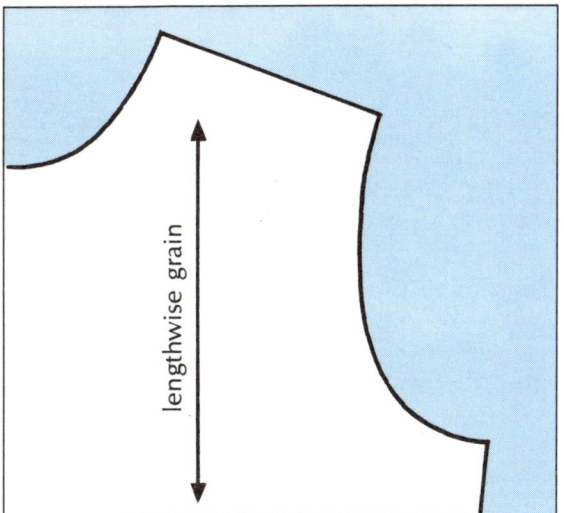

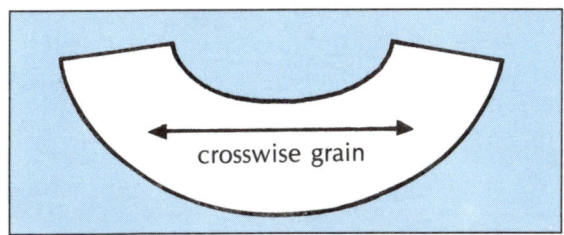

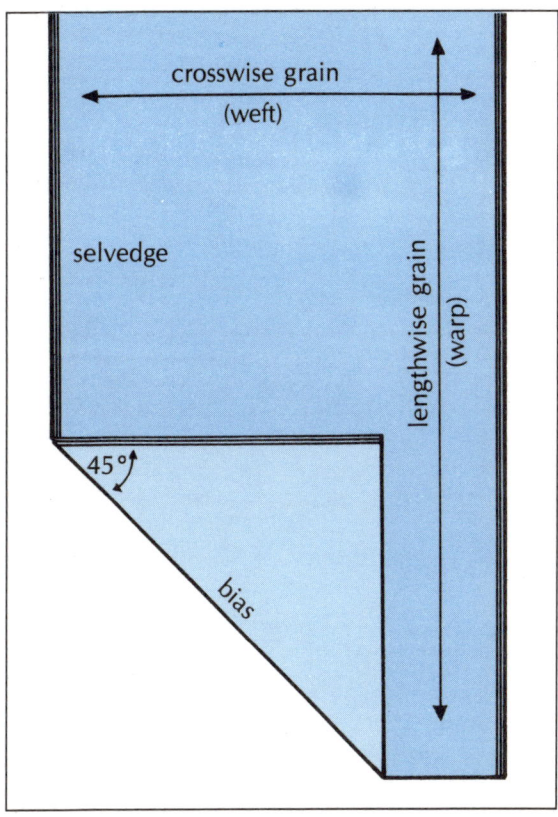

angle. The fold line shows where the stretch of the material is.

Cutting line

The heavy dark line marking your size.

Fold line

The marking where there is no seam line.

Seam line

The pattern shows a broken line.

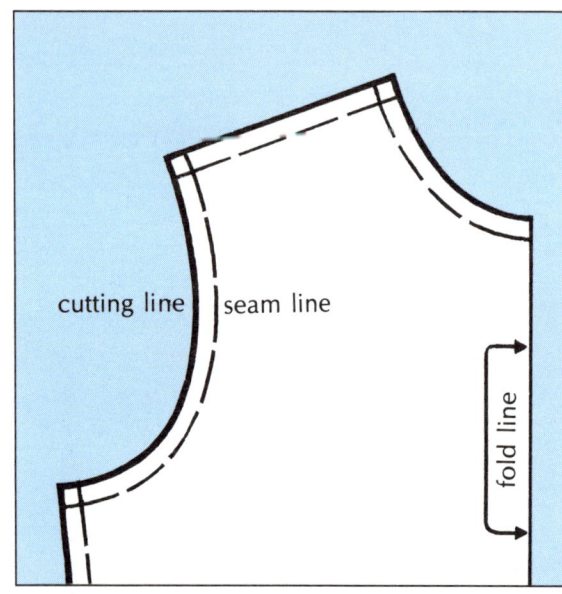

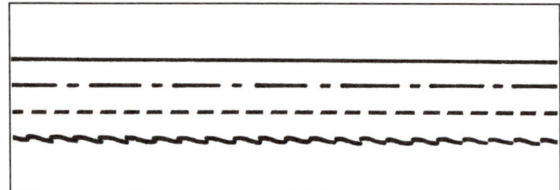

Different ways of indicating seam lines

Buttonhole position

Sometimes there is a separate strip of pattern with buttonhole markings which you lay on your garment to mark the distance between buttonholes.

Notches

Small V-shaped nicks for matching pattern pieces, which help keep the material on the correct grainline. Never cut too deeply into the seam line when cutting notches. (On sleeve pieces only, one notch indicates the front of a pattern piece, two notches the back.)

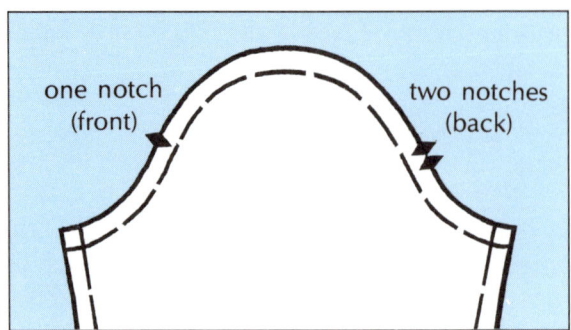

Tailor tacks

Thread markings indicating openings for zips, dart placements and other features which need marking once the pattern piece is removed from the cut fabric.

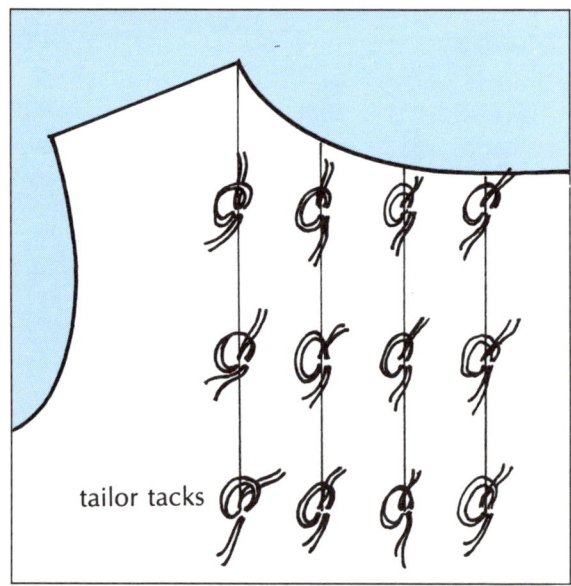

Button position

A cross indicating where a button is to be sewn. Make sure it lines up with the buttonhole position.

Pleat position

Arrows point in the direction the pleat has to be folded. Usually a fold follows an unbroken line marking going towards a broken line.

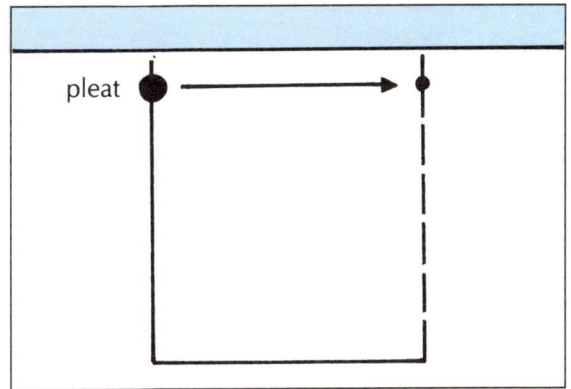

The toile

A toile is a calico 'practice' copy of the garment you intend to make. Using this you can perfect the pattern before cutting out your fabric. Darts and seam lines can be marked on the toile with biro to help give a correct fitting.

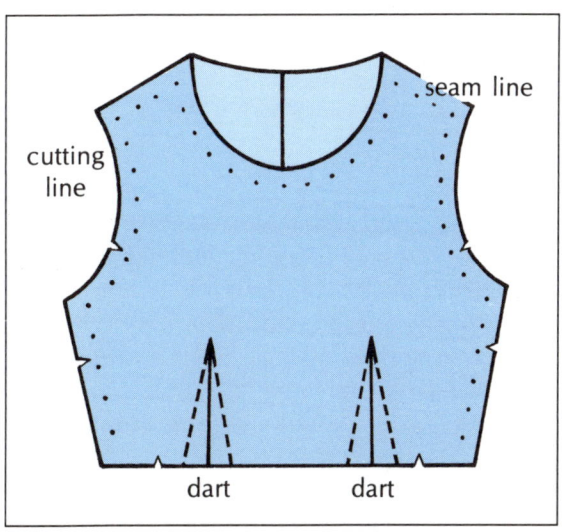

A toile ready for the cutting stage

Cutting out

1. On the guide sheet supplied with the pattern, circle the correct pattern layout for your size and the width of your material.
2. Press pattern pieces with a warm iron so they will lie flat.
3. Cut around the pattern pieces on the heavy black line. If more than one size is included on the pattern piece, pin through the pattern to the fabric on your size line. Lift the pattern slightly and mark at the pin line with tailor's chalk before cutting.
4. Make any necessary alterations to pattern pieces to suit your fitting. To shorten a piece, fold on adjustment line and pin. To lengthen, cut along the adjustment line and add a plain piece of paper the required length. Tape in place.
5. Press the fabric to remove any creases before pinning pattern pieces in place.
6. Use a pin to mark the right side of the fabric. This saves time when assembling the garment. The width of the fabric will determine which layout to use. Patterns have a 'Cutting Layout Shading Key' chart. Check this and follow as you pin the pattern pieces on the fabric.
7. Start placing the pins from the top of the pattern pieces and work downwards, pressing any creases down towards the bottom as you continue pinning.
8. Transfer all tissue markings to fabric before removing pattern, e.g. cutting notches, marking darts and circles with tailor's chalk.
9. Keep one hand on the pattern pieces while cutting out. Keep material lying flat.

Tacking *(illustrated on page 33)*

Tacking is used when you start to join two pieces of material together. Tacking gives you a guide to match all your nicks and seams evenly. It also stops your material moving off the grainline. Use a single thread with a knot at the end, in the same colour as the fabric. Cheaper cottons can be used for tacking to cut cost.

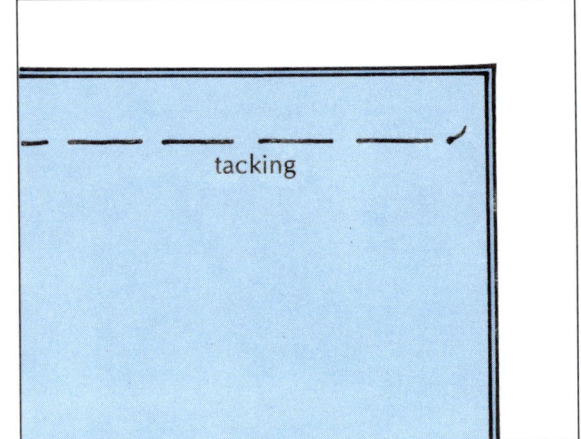

1. Sew 1 cm stitches evenly in and out of the fabric.
2. To remove tacking threads, cut individual stitches and pull out gently. Do not pull several stitches at once, or a very long thread, as this can cause puckering of the fabric.

Remember to pin straight, tack straight and sew straight.

Basting *(illustrated on page 33)*

Basting is a form of tacking used when you need to treat two layers of fabric as one so they will not move from the grainline. It is also used when interfacing is sewn into a garment. Thread a single thread, no knot. Make long slanting stitches 5 cm apart across the fabrics, taking care to keep the fabrics flat. Leave a tiny tail of cotton at the end of each line for removing the basting. Because these stitches are so much larger than tacking stitches, they can be safely pulled out—but gently.

Tailor tacks *(illustrated on page 33)*

Tailor tacks are thread markings used instead of pins. They are very useful on patterned materials where pins may be difficult to see clearly, and also on sheer or delicate fabrics which pins can damage or slide out of easily.

1. Use a double strand of coloured thread.
2. Sew a loop over the symbol you want to transfer.
3. Cut through the loop, and remove the pattern tissue.

Tailor tack thread markings are useful on patterned material when it is difficult to see pins clearly

Seams

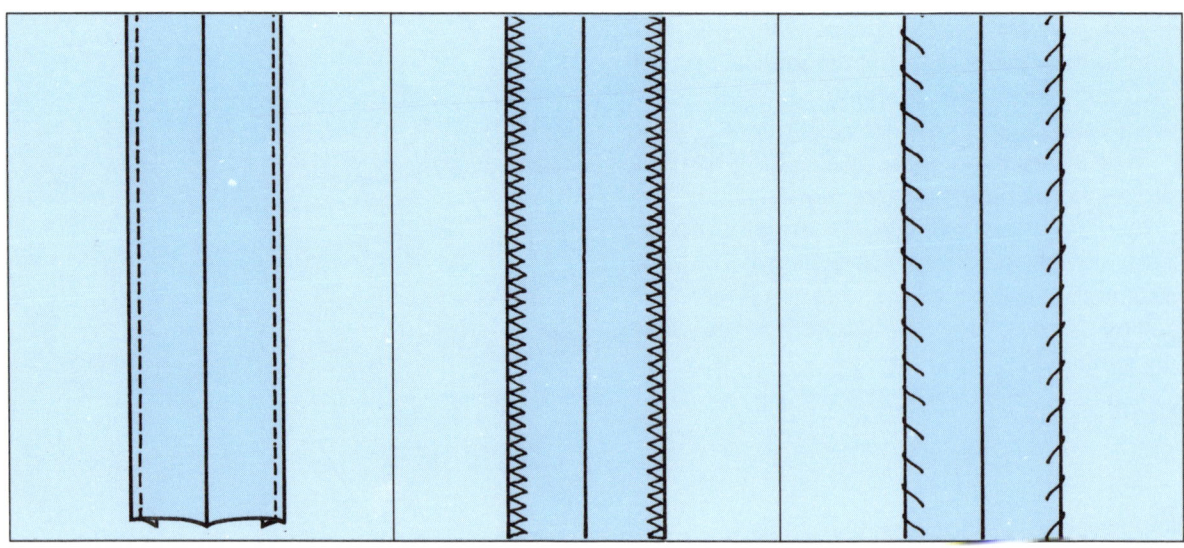

Stitched and turned seam   *Zigzagged seam*   *Overcast seam*

Stitched and turned seam

(illustrated on page 33)

This is a neat tailored finish for light to medium weight fabrics. Even with the recent arrival of overlockers on the market for home sewers, the stitched and turned seam is still a very good neat finish. The trick is to get the right balance between thread tension and fabric weight. If the tension is wrong, puckering may appear along the seam. Work a test sample first.

1. With right sides of material facing together, pin, tack and machine along the seam line.
2. Press the seam open and flat; the two raw edges are folded down 6 mm and machine-stitched close to the edge.

Zigzagged seam

This machine finish is more suitable on heavier weight fabrics such as broadcloth and corduroy, and on some woollen-mixture fabrics.

1. Trim the seam allowance after machining the seam.
2. Change the machine needle to a heavy duty one; this will help the tension. Set stitch for medium width.
3. Turn knob for zigzagging and sew close to the edge.
4. You must have the right tension to prevent gathering.
5. Zig-zag seams are practical for woollen or thicker fabrics, providing no stretching or gathering occurs.

Hand-sewn overcast seam

This finish will prevent fraying when sewing a very soft fabric, where machining and zigzag are not suitable and could cause puckering.

1. Press the seam flat open.
2. Thread a fine sewing needle with a single matching thread and a small knot at the end.
3. Starting at the top of the seam, sew diagonal stitches over the edge of the fabric, spacing the stitches evenly apart. Take care to catch the garment into the stitching.
4. Keep your stitches flat to prevent pulling.
5. Using a press-cloth and a warm iron, press seams flat.

French seam
(illustrated on page 33)

French seams are suitable for both fine and sheer see-through fabrics. They look neat and prevent fraying. They are very practical for clothes that are laundered frequently, especially babywear and children's clothes.

1. Place wrong sides of fabric together (first stitching will be machined on the right side of the fabric).
2. Pin, tack and machine a narrow 13 mm seam.
3. Trim evenly to 6 mm wide.
4. Fold the seam over (roll the edge of the seam with your fingers) and press flat. Tack again just below the raw edges encased inside.
5. Check no threads are on view before machining.
6. Press seam flat.

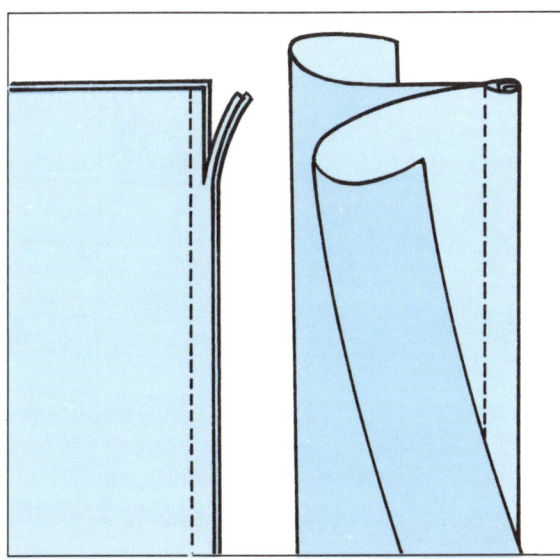

Run and fell seam (flat-felled)
(illustrated on page 34)

This is a very sturdy external finish, very practical for sportswear, children's clothes and jeans. Using a contrasting colour thread can make a decorative finish, e.g. red cotton on navy material.

1,2,3. Start by following and machining steps 1, 2 and 3 as in the French seam instructions.
4. The next step constructs the run and fell seam:
5. The folded edge on the wrong side of the material is machined through to the right side of the garment, with matching or a contrasting colour thread.

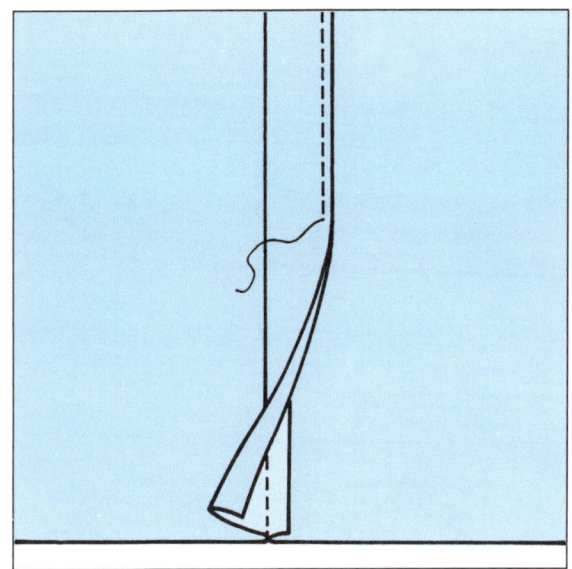

Hong Kong seam

Hong Kong seams have bias strips made from a soft fabric sewn to the edges. Matching ready-made bias binding can be used also. Very neat, this seam reduces bulk on woollen and heavier weight fabrics, and is very suitable for unlined garments.

1. Stitch seam and press seam flat open.
2. With right sides of bias binding and right side of seam edge, machine a 6 mm seam.
3. Press fold over to the underside.
4. On the right side, stitch in the crevice of the fold.

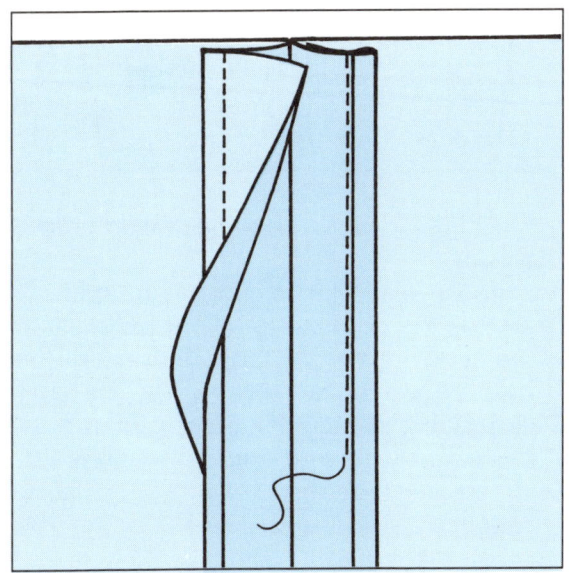

Facings *(illustrated on page 34)*

All facings on a garment, e.g. neckline, front and back neck openings, must line up perfectly after being sewn to the garment. Any sign of pulling or puckering means the garment will lose its professional finish. Match all nicks and symbols, always tack in place, be careful not to stretch.

1. Join the front and back facings right sides together at the shoulder seams. Press the seams flat open.

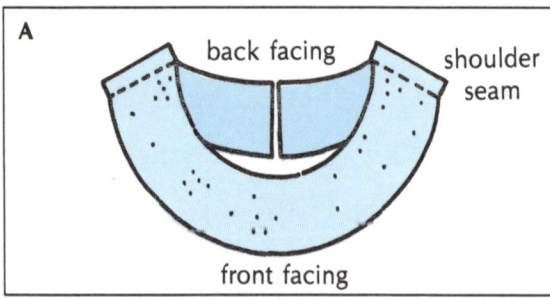

2. With right sides of facing and garment together and matching shoulder and neck seams, pin and tack around neckline.

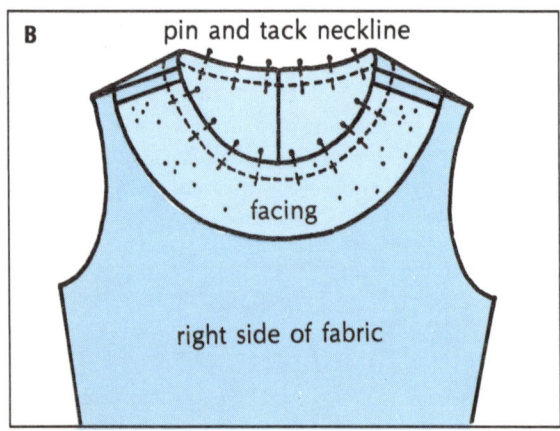

3. Machine around neckline and remove tacking.
4. Trim the seam and nick it 6 mm apart all around the neckline to help it to lie flat in the curved areas. Be careful not to cut too deeply towards the stitching line (Fig.C).
5. Turn facing to the inside of the garment, roll the seams with your fingers and press flat.
6. Understitch the seam allowance to the facing (see next page) (Fig.D).

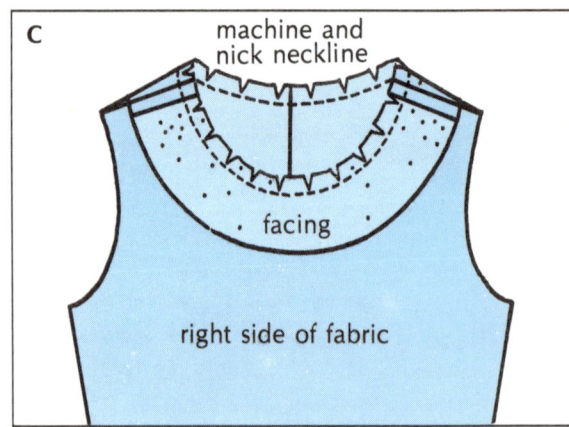

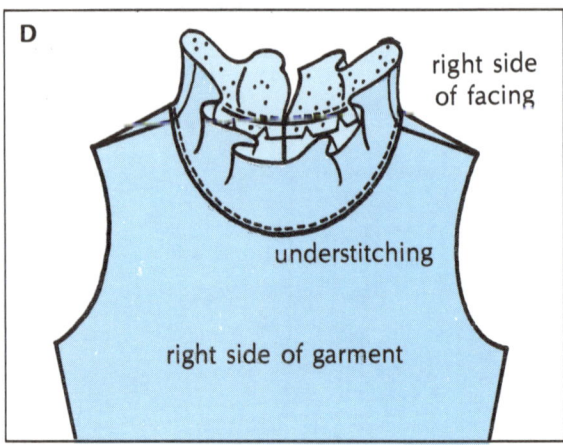

7. Neaten the raw edges of the facing by turning and machining close to the edge.
8. Holding a shoulder pad underneath the facing, press it flat. This helps to prevent stitching the neckline.
9. On the wrong side of the garment, slipstitch the facing to the shoulder seam.

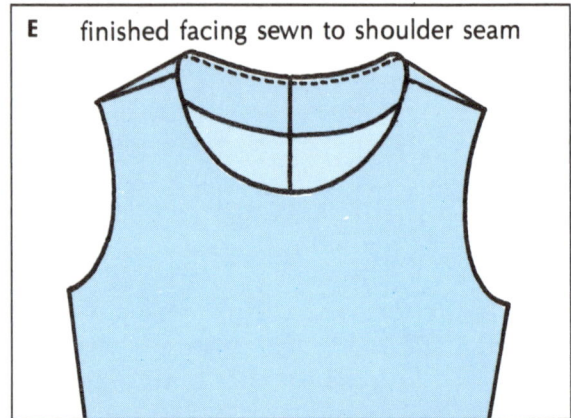

Interfacing

Interfacing, an extra layer of fabric, provides extra support, helps the shape and prevents stretching. The type of interfacing you choose depends on the garment fabric. Interfacing is available in light, medium and heavy grades, in both sew-in and iron-on types. The non-iron or sew-in interfacing is usually set into woollen or similar, heavier weight fabrics, the iron-on type being better for lightweight fabrics.

Interfacing is used in collars, front or back openings, lapels, waistbands, pockets and some pocket flaps. Its use is illustrated on pages 30 and 41.

1. Always follow the pattern instructions for a particular garment.
2. If using the iron-on type, trim seam allowance before fusing to avoid unnecessary bulk.
4. Sew-in interfacing is basted in place to prevent it moving from the grainline. The garment section and the interfacing are then treated as one piece.

Understitching

Understitching keeps facings and seam lines from rolling to the right side of the garment. Always trim and remove any bulk from seam allowances before understitching.

1. To understitch a facing around the neckline of a garment, pull facing out flat and on the right side machine close to the seam line and through the seam allowance underneath. This stitch is not visible on the main part of the garment.
2. When understitching collars, cut the seam allowance along edge to eliminate bulk. Turn the collars inside out and, as far as possible, understitch on the wrong side of the collar.
3. Side pockets in skirts or frocks will stop pulling out if a row of understitching is machined as far down on the straight sections as possible, before the curving area of the pocket.

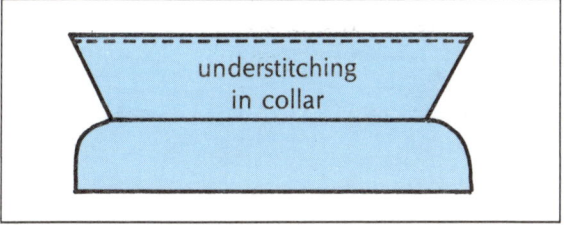

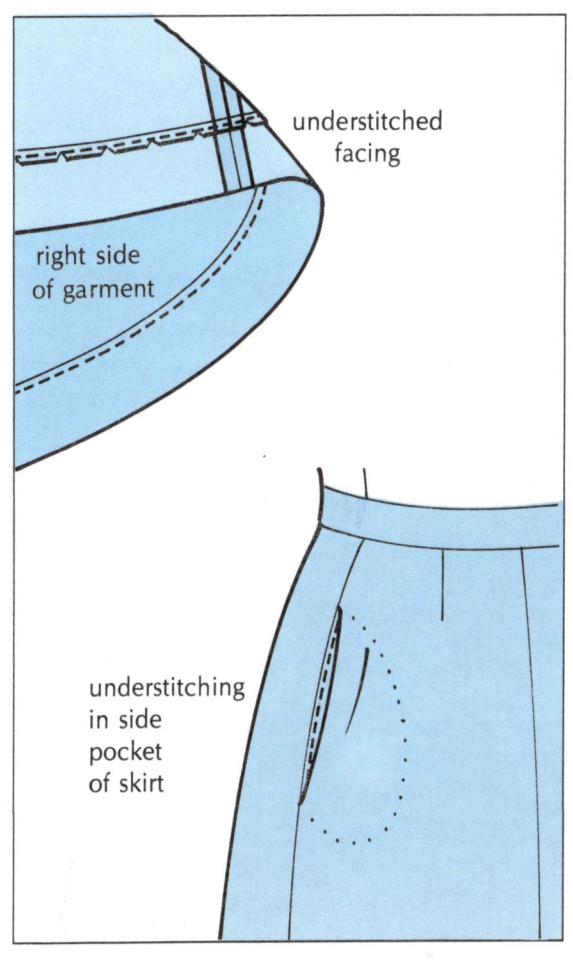

Topstitching

Topstitching is a technique to keep edges and seams flat and to help pleats hang smoothly. Stitching is worked from the right side of the garment through all thicknesses of fabric. The best method is to topstitch each section during the construction of the garment. A contrasting thread makes a decorative feature.

1. Pin pleats in place on right side of garment (Fig.A).
2. Tack pleats from top down and 13 mm in from pleat edge (Fig.B).
3. Pin each pleat at the point where the topstitching will begin.
4. Stitch from bottom up towards the top, with the edge of the machine foot running level with the edge of the garment (Fig.C).
5. Pull thread through to wrong side and tie (Fig.D).

Knife-pleated skirt

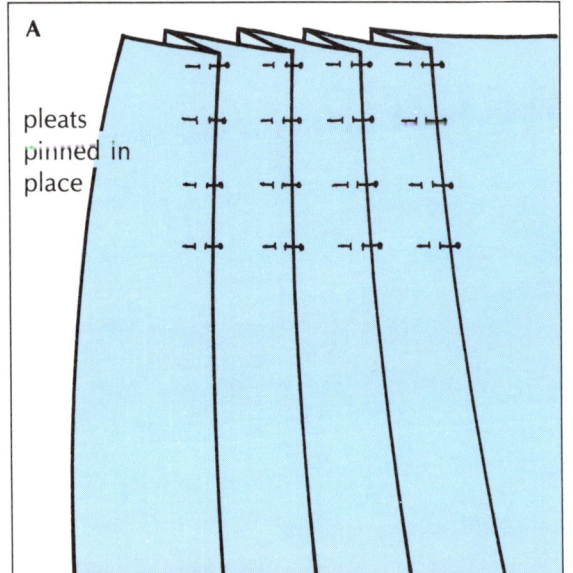

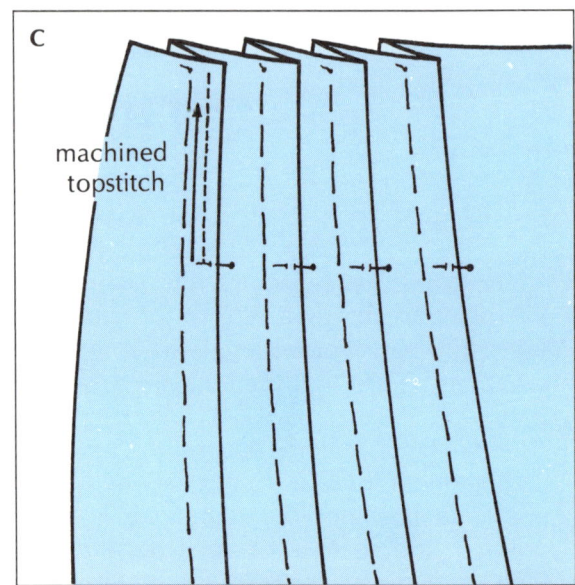

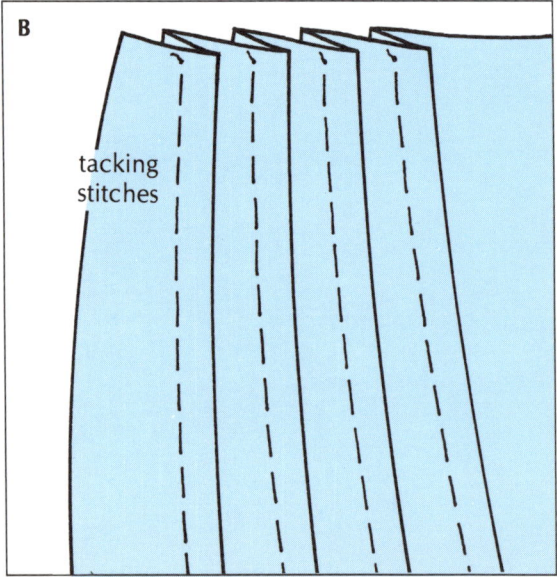

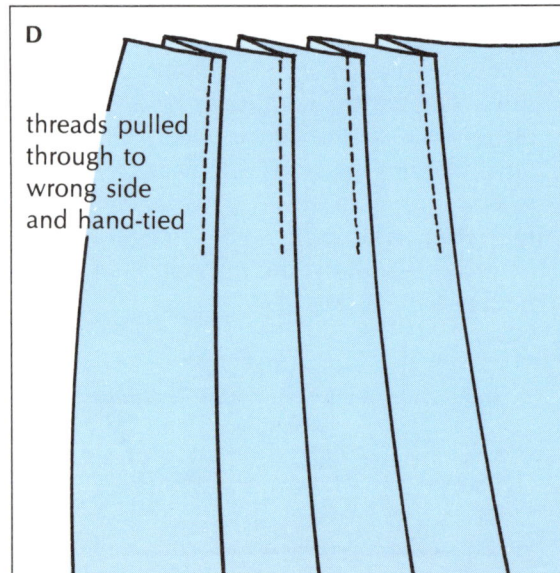

Peter Pan collar

1. Complete collar from instructions.
2. On the right side of the collar, outline with a marking pencil the exact width for topstitching.
3. Change machine needle to a heavy duty size (the point of the needle is finer and will penetrate all the layers more easily).
4. Increase stitch length. Check the Needle and Thread Chart on page 12 for the correct thread to prevent puckering of the garment.
5. When machining in the deep collar (strongly curved) area, it is helpful to pivot around the curves. Keep the machine needle down in the fabric, lift the pressure foot and turn slightly, lower foot and continue stitching to end of collar. This can be repeated several times.

Jackets

1. The pattern for a topstitched jacket will stipulate the step-by-step stages of the construction of the jacket.
2. Before sewing, check the Needle and Thread Chart on page 12 for the correct thread to use on your fabric. Change to a heavy duty needle and make stitch length a little longer than usual to accommodate extra thicknesses.
3. Before topstitching remove any bulk from seams and interfacings to keep the right side of the garment even and flat.

Pointed collar

1. Follow the instructions for the Peter Pan collar.
2. You will only need to pivot once, at each corner.

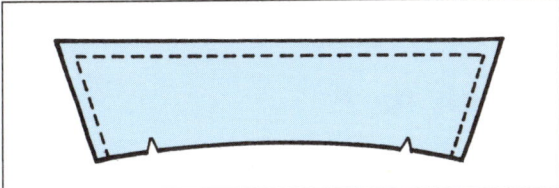

Darts

Darts help mould a flat piece of material to the convex human shape. They also control and direct fullness. Darts are used at the bustline, back bodice, waist and hip areas.

Bodice darts

1. Before removing the pattern from the fabric, pin through the circle markings representing the darts on the wrong side of the fabric.
2. Lift the pattern up and mark the pin positions with tailor's chalk.

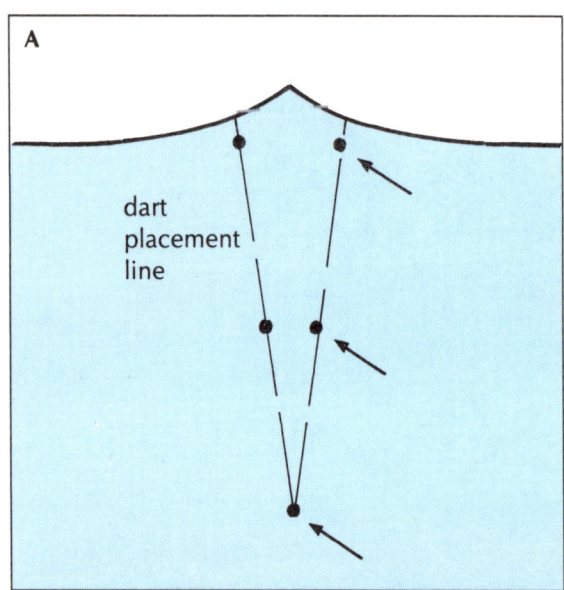

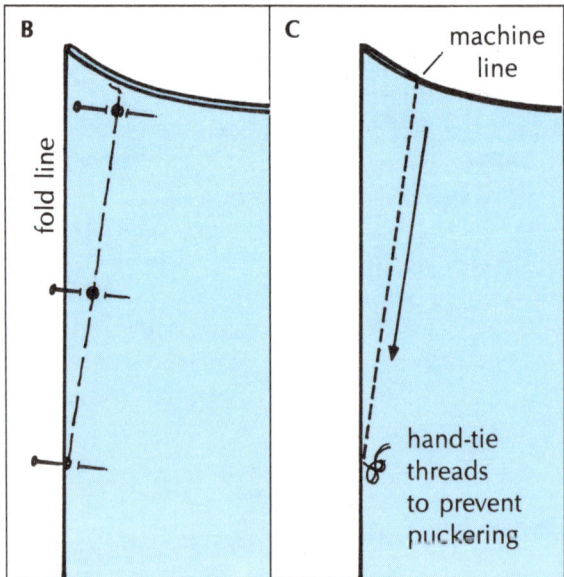

3. Fold the dart in half with the right sides of the fabric together, matching the chalk markings. Tailor tacks can also be used as a guide (Fig.B).
4. Press lightly along the foldline before stitching. This will help the dart to lie flat. Tack in place.
5. Always sew from the top of the dart down to the tip, *never* in the opposite direction. Do not reverse stitch at the end, but hand-knot the bottom threads to prevent puckering (Fig.C).
6. Press darts flat on an ironing board. Refer back to the pattern guidesheet to see in which direction each dart is to lie after pressing (Fig.D).

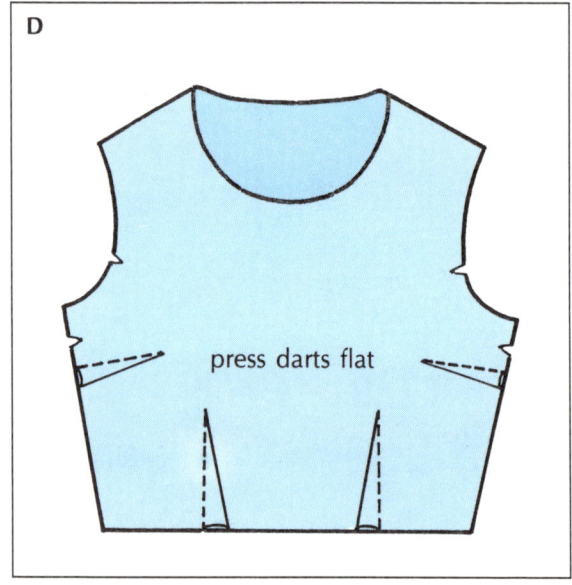

French darts

French darts are curved. They help to shape the waistline area where a garment has no waistline seam. French darts are only used in the front of a garment, never at the back.

1. Chalk the circle markings from the pattern onto the fabric and pin and tack in place on wrong side.

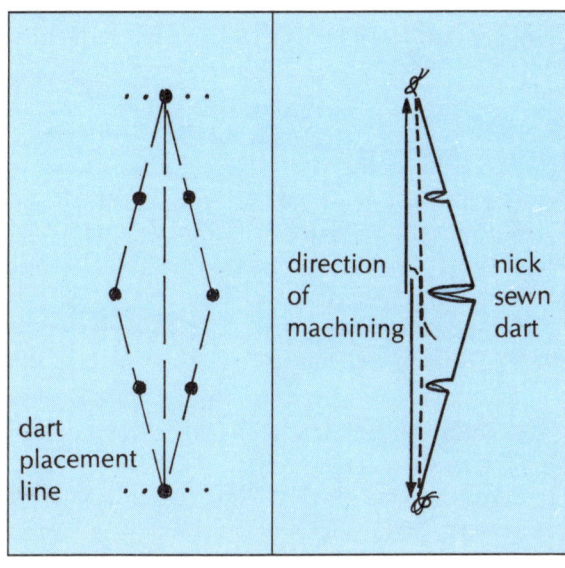

to cut too close to the point or fraying will occur.
4. Clip seam allowance to let curve lie flat. Press flat.

Contour darts

A contour dart is a long single dart, double-ended. Its widest point fits at the waistline, then the dart tapers in both directions.

1. Chalk the circle markings from the pattern in place on the wrong side of the fabric.
2. Fold dart in half, matching chalk markings. Pin and tack in place.
3. Machine from the middle of the dart to one end. Go back to the middle and stitch to the other point. Tie thread ends and remove tacking.
4. Clip dart at waistline and each side. Press flat.

2. Machine dart from end to point, and hand-knot thread ends. Do not machine-reverse at the end. Remove tacking.
3. Cut through the centre of the dart, from the wide end almost to the point. Be careful not

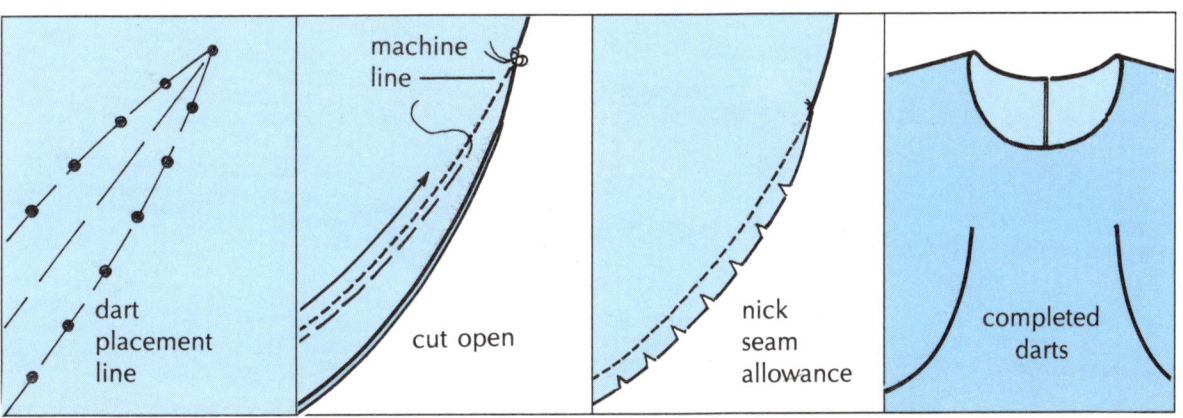

Bias strips

A bias cut is made when the fabric is cut on the diagonal, at 45° to the lengthwise and crosswise threads. Fabric cut on the true bias has maximum 'give', which helps shape garments. Avoid stretching the fabric when working with bias-cut pieces, and follow carefully all pattern markings.

Although commercial bias binding is readily available, bias binding made from the same fabric as the garment looks more professional, as everything matches. Remember that the inside of your garment should be as neat as the outside.

1. Fold a square or rectangle of fabric on the true diagonal, with the threads lining up exactly on the lengthwise and crosswise grains.

2. Cut along fold to make the first cutting line. Before you go further remember that a strip of bias fabric 38 mm wide is suitable for most items (Fig.B).
3. To join bias strips, put right sides together, straight-grain raw edges together. Slide across until strips cross approximately 1 cm from corners. Stitch on straight grain from corner to corner (Fig.C).
4. Trim seam to 75 mm. Press open. Working from the right side of bias strip, press a narrow hem each side (Fig.D).
5. Press the strip evenly in half down the middle. The bias binding is now ready to be used on a garment (Fig.E).

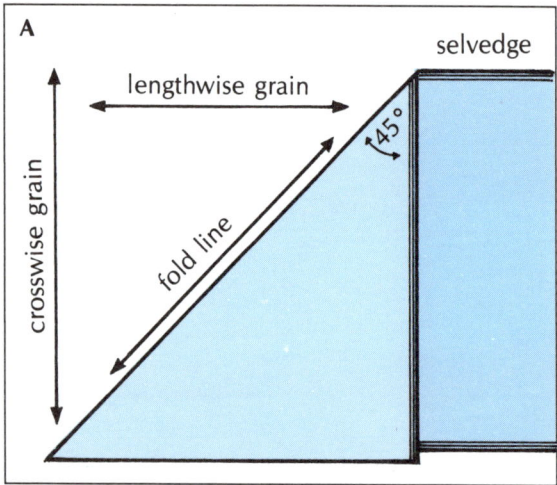

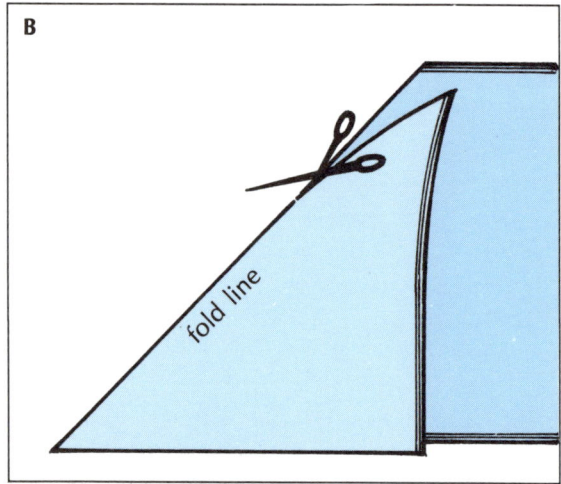

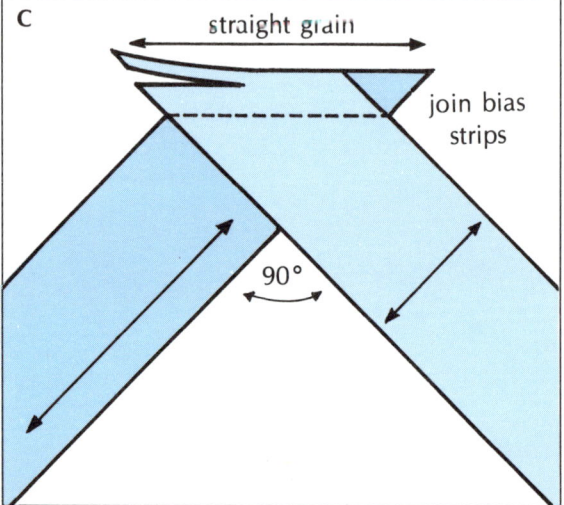

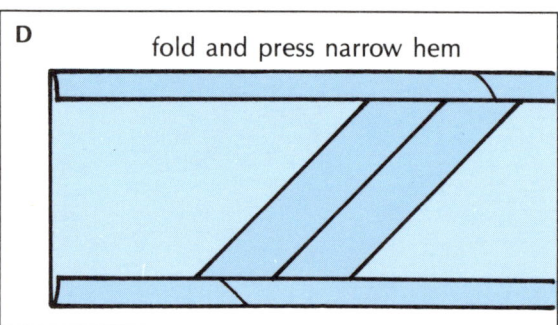

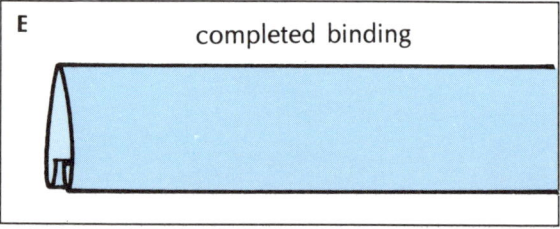

Bindings *(illustrated on page 34)*

Double binding

Bindings are a neat and practical finish around necklines or sleeveless armholes. Made in a contrast colour they can give a very attractive finish. Make sure if you are using a colour contrast that the binding fabric is the same texture as the main fabric. This way the tension of the materials will be even and the bindings will lie flat. Check whether the fabric should be pre-washed to prevent shrinking later on.

1. Measure the length of the area you are binding; allow 25 mm for seam allowance.
2. Cut bias strip 31 mm wide.
3. With wrong sides together, press the binding in half.
4. When binding a neckline, make the join at the shoulder; never make a join in the front or the back of the neckline. Armhole bindings should join at the sideseam under the arm.
5. Pin the binding on the right side of the garment, tack and machine along the seam line. Remove tacking.

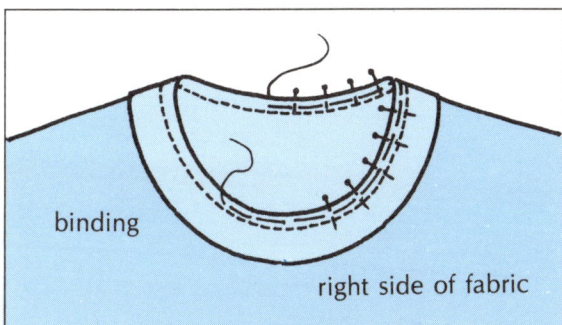

6. Trim seam allowance evenly and press the binding strip up towards the top.

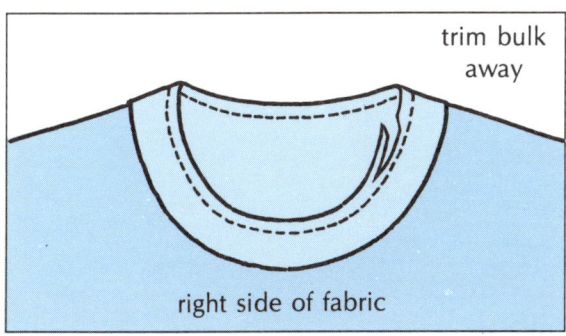

7. Flip the binding over the raw edge to the wrong side of the garment. This forms what is called a 'wall' and must stand upright. Slipstitch a hem on the raw edge of the binding.

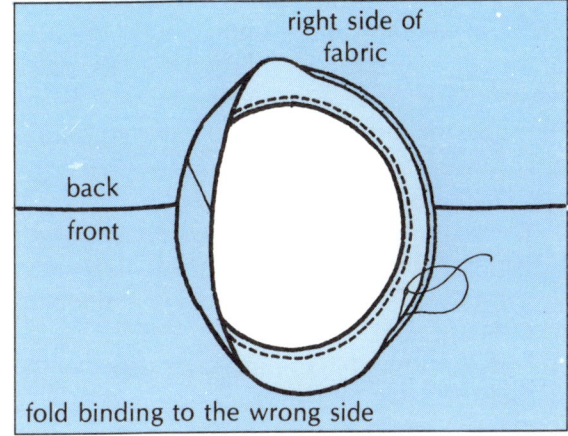

8. On the right side of the garment, pin in the ditch, which means in the gutter of the seam directly below the wall. Tack in place with matching thread; use bigger stitches at the back, as they are easier to remove.
9. Change the sewing machine foot to a zipper foot; this makes it easier to sew in the ditch and not on the binding. Remove tacking from back, cutting thread away.

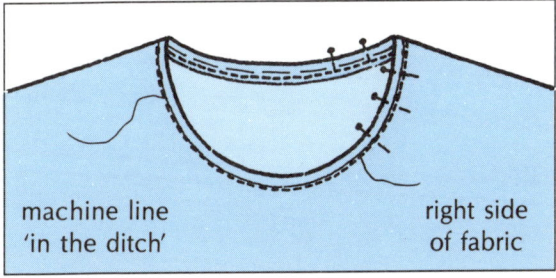

10. Hold a shoulder pad under binding and press with a warm iron.

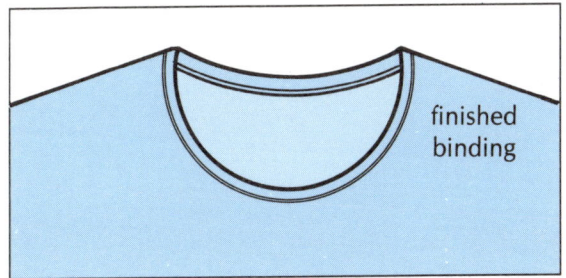

Rouleaus

Rouleaus are ties or cylindrical strips of fabric. They are made from strips of material cut on the bias, which after machining are pulled through themselves to form ties. They are used for shoulder straps, and are traditionally used for the loops that fasten covered buttons on the backs of wedding and evening gowns in place of zipper openings. Hand-stitched into daisy flower shapes and beaded with tiny seed beads they give millinery, gowns and crafts a fashionable finish.

1. To make shoulder straps, measure the length required for the strap plus a seam allowance.
2. Cut bias strips 25 mm wide and the length required.
3. Fold the strip in half, right sides together, so that the edges are even.
4. Stitch a 6 mm seam along its length.
5. Thread a darning needle with fancywork cotton; for strength, make a small knot at the end.
6. Sew thread through end of strip to fasten.
7. Insert the eye of the needle into the strip and slide it through to the other end. Gently pull through to the end, cut off thread. Do not press rouleaus.

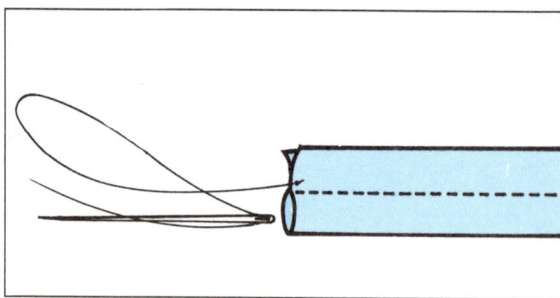

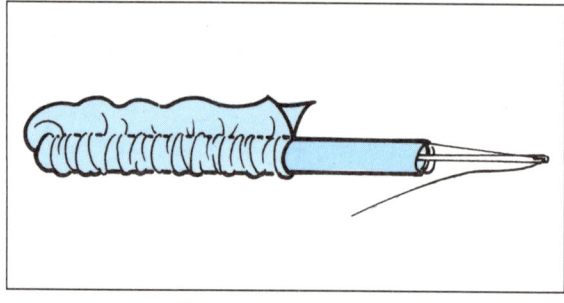

Gathering

Gathering in a garment helps control fullness. It is used at waistlines and cuffs, sometimes in yokes and for making frills.

1. With the stitch length set at maximum, machine two lines of gathering stitches just above the seam line.

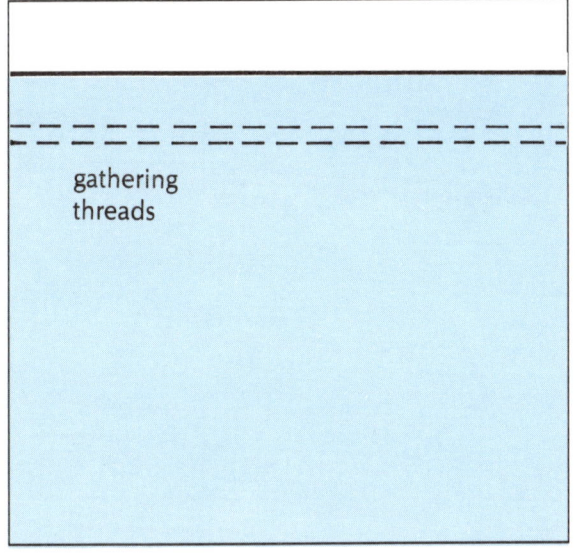

2. Insert a strong pin under a stitch and pull the thread up, then slide the fabric along the thread. Continue in this manner until all the gathers are even. It is easier to pull the gathering thread at intervals along the fabric than to pull the thread from end to end, as often it will snap.

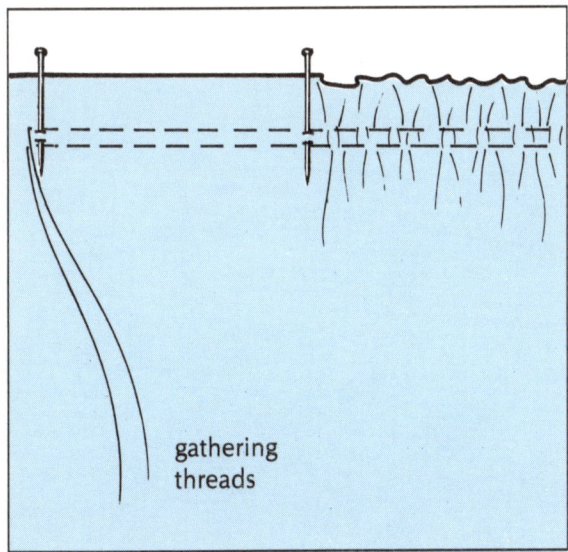

3. To join the gathered section to another part of the garment, place the pins vertically, tack in place, then machine. Remove the tacking.

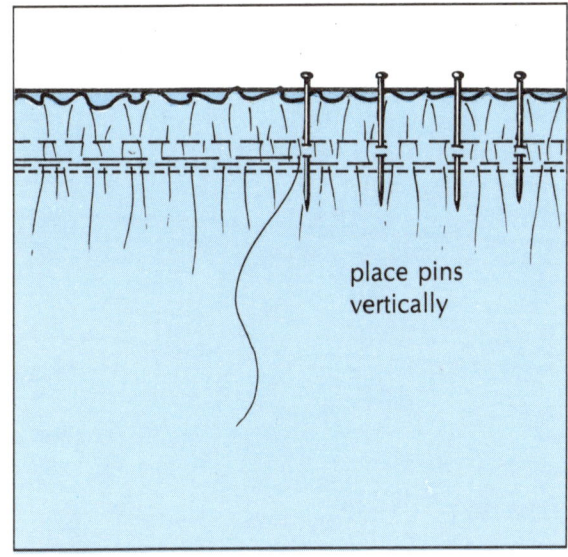

4. Press the gathers by working the point of the iron between the folds. Do not press across the gathers, as this flattens them.

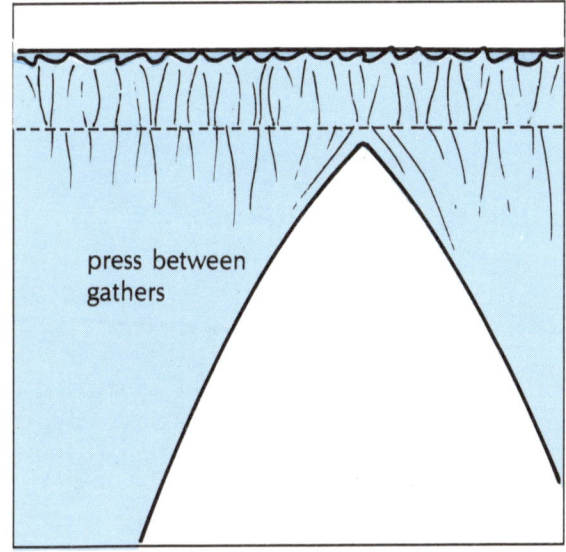

Collars

Collars can add a particular fashion note to a garment. They are at eye contact level so finished detail must be exact. Pattern guides usually advise the correct interfacings to use with different fabrics. Interfacing is important, as it gives the added support needed for a professional finish. Corners and curves also can make or break a collar. Eliminate bulk in the seams by trimming the seam allowance from the interfacing before it is applied to the collar.

Pointed collar

1. Cut the iron-on interfacing pieces from the directions on the pattern guide sheet.
2. Trim away all seam allowances on interfacing to reduce bulk and press onto collar.

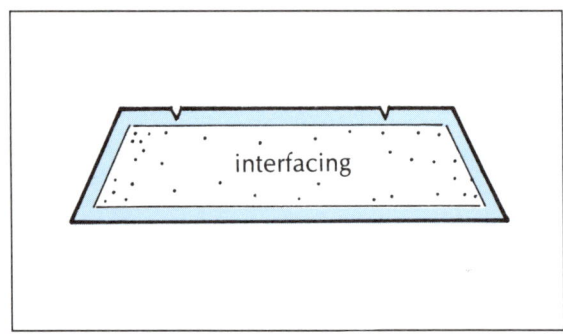

3. Join collar pieces with right sides facing together. Pin and tack in place on seam line and machine stitch.

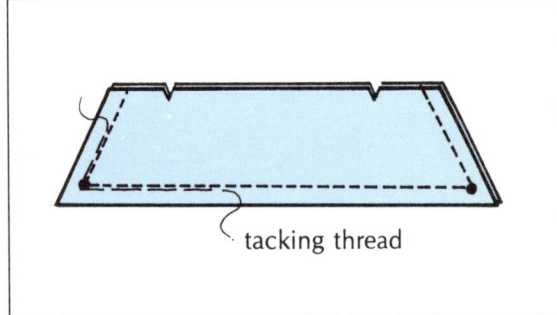

4. Trim seam edges and cut corners on an angle to remove bulk.

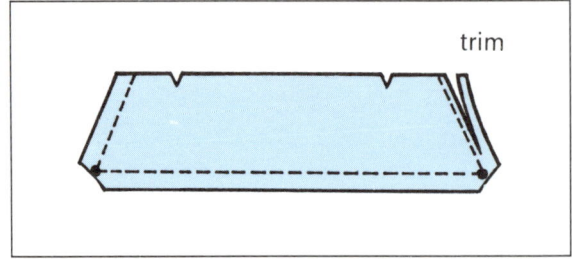

5. Turn collar to right side and roll seam with your fingers. Press collar.

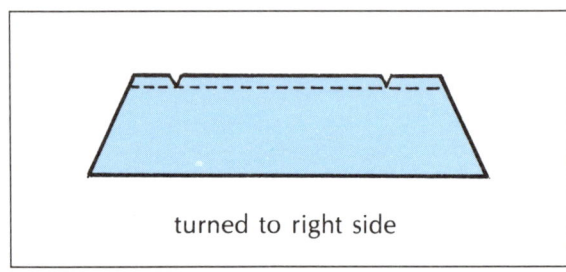

6. The collar is now ready to be fitted to your garment. Follow the pattern instructions carefully, and *always* tack in place.

Peter Pan collar
(illustrated on page 35)

The method outlined for the pointed collar applies to the Peter Pan collar, except that the rounded corners have to be nicked completely

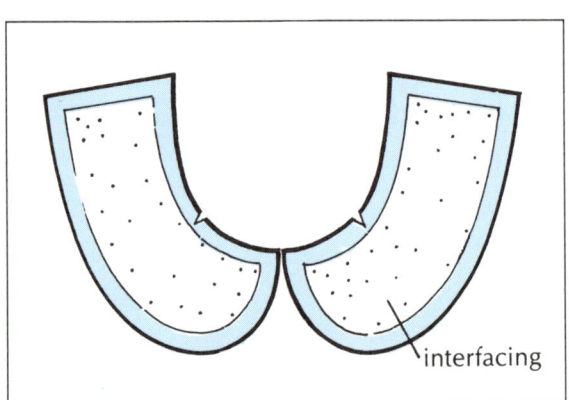

around the curves to make the collar hang perfectly flat. On the straight section of the collar sew a row of understitching. Press through each stage.

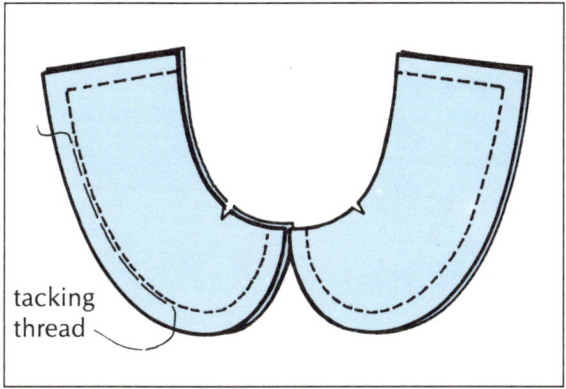

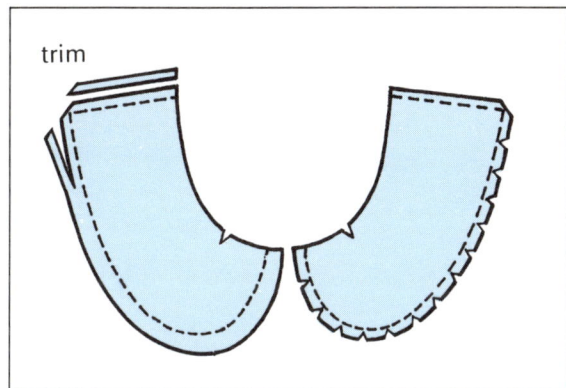

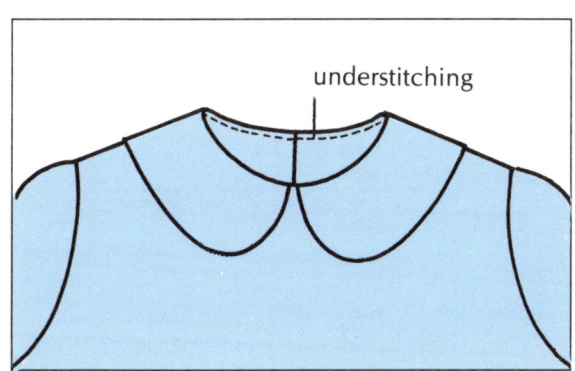

Shirt collar
(illustrated on page 35)

A shirt collar has a section called a collar stand. This section lies between the shirt and the collar and allows space for a tie to be worn. Some women's blouses also have a collar stand. They are a particularly smart finish to a blouse.

1. Follow pointed collar instructions from 1 to 5.
2. Apply interfacing to the wrong side of the collar stand piece.

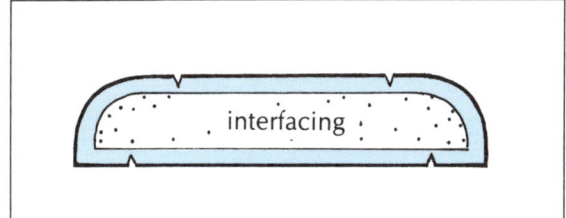

3. With right sides of the stand facing together, pin and tack between the two circle markings on the curved ends of the stand. Machine, trim curves and turn to the right side. Press flat.

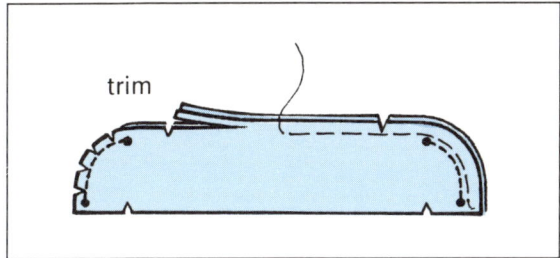

4. With the right sides of the upper collar toward the right side of the stand's facing, match and pin the collar to the stand. Tack through all thicknesses along seamline. Machine, remove tacking and turn to right side. Press flat.

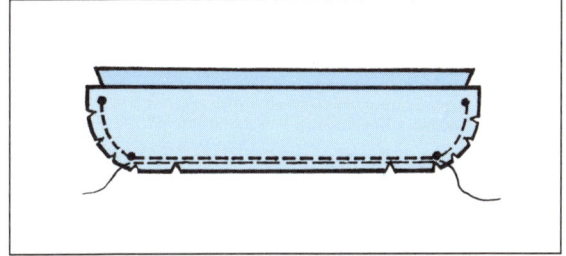

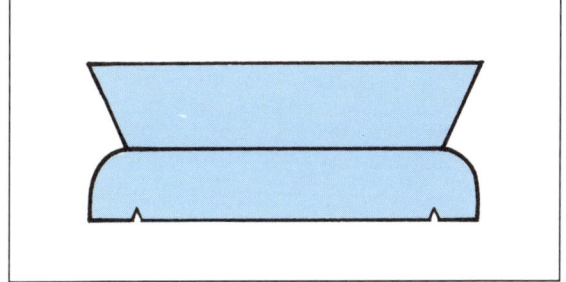

5. The collar is now ready to be stitched to the neckline. Follow instructions carefully.

Cuffs

Cuffs can give added flair to a garment. A basic black frock with contrasting white cuffs and collar can look extremely smart. Where the cuffs are joined with buttons, adding a buttonhole either side of the cuff and holding them together with cuff links can be an added fashion touch. Most cuffs open wider with a placket set into the sleeve.

Placket

1. Cut a bias fabric binding 40 mm wide and twice the length of the marked placket on the sleeve, following the instructions on page 26.
2. Machine a V-shaped row of stitching on the seamline where the opening has to be cut in the sleeve. Cut to the end of the opening.

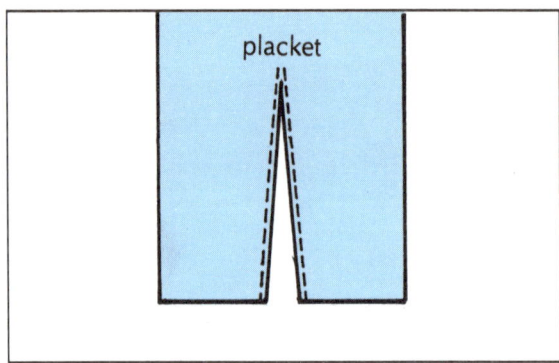

3. With right sides of sleeve and bindings facing together, pin and tack along placket opening, machine, remove tacking and press seam flat.

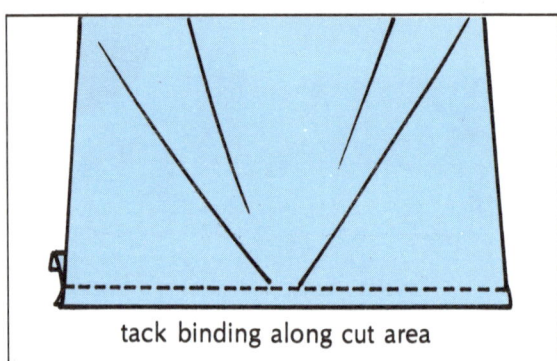
tack binding along cut area

4. Fold binding to the wrong side, encasing raw edges. Fold the edge of the binding to meet the stitching line. Pin in place, tack, and machine close to the edge, removing tacking.

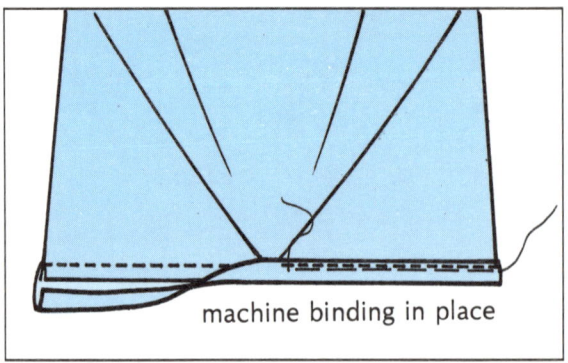
machine binding in place

5. Turn binding to wrong side of sleeve and press.

Cuff

1. Cut iron-on interfacing half the depth of the cuff, press in place on wrong side.

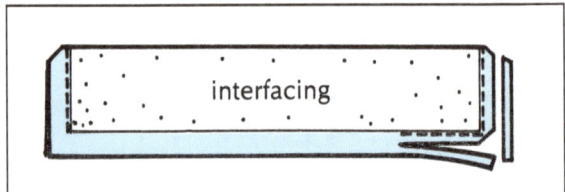

2. Fold cuff in half, right sides together.
3. At the right-hand end, machine down 4 cm, then across 4 cm. This is the section for the buttonhole. Trim the seam and cut seam corners on an angle to remove bulk.
4. At the end of the cuff machine a 1.5 cm seam.
5. At the end of the overlap (buttonhole) section, cut up a little and turn cuff to the right side. Press flat.

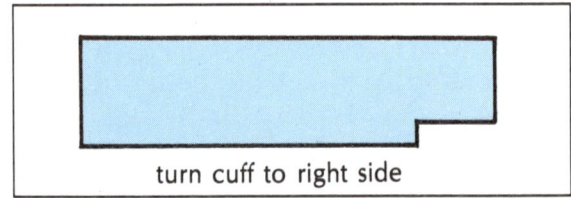
turn cuff to right side

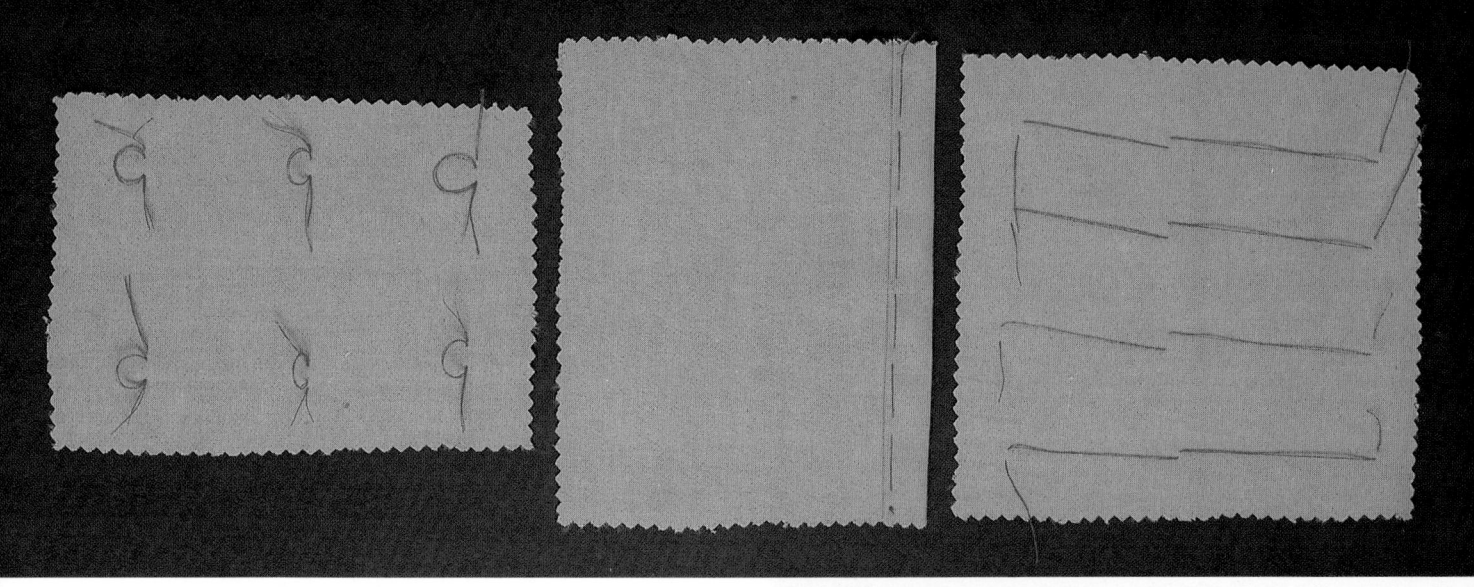

Left to right: tailor tacks (page 17), tacking (page 16) and basting (page 17)

Stages in making a French seam (page 19)

Stitched and turned seam (page 18)

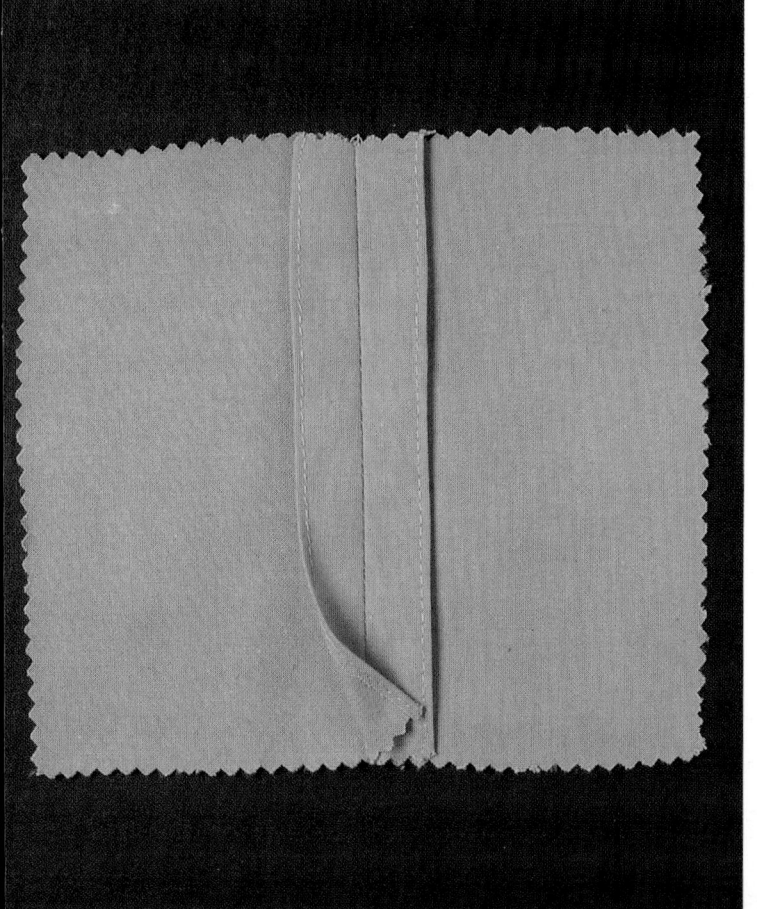

Stages in making a run and fell seam (page 19)

Stages in making the facing for a neckline (page 20)

Steps in binding a neckline (page 27)

Making a Peter Pan collar (page 30)

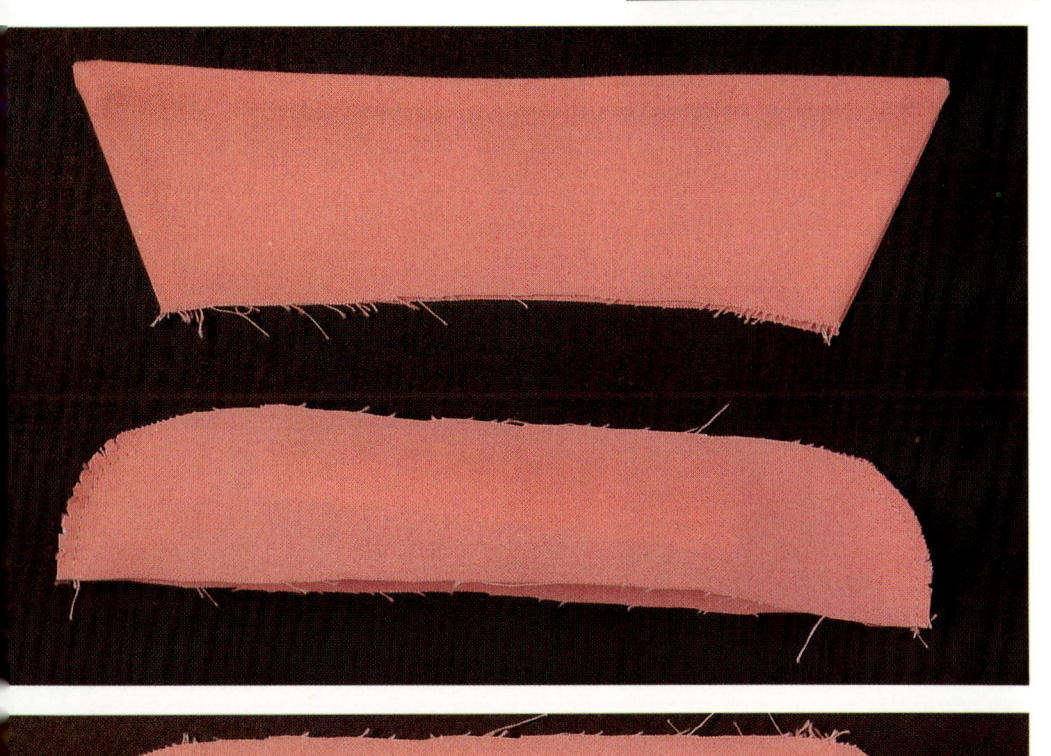

Stages in making a shirt collar with collar stand (page 31)

35

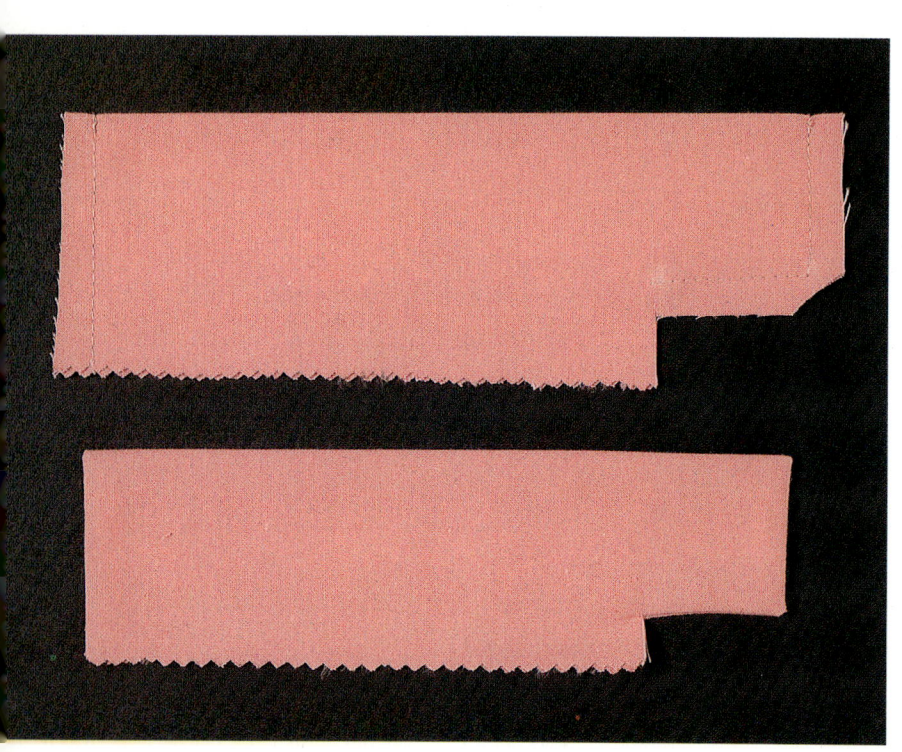

The first steps in making a waistband (page 41)

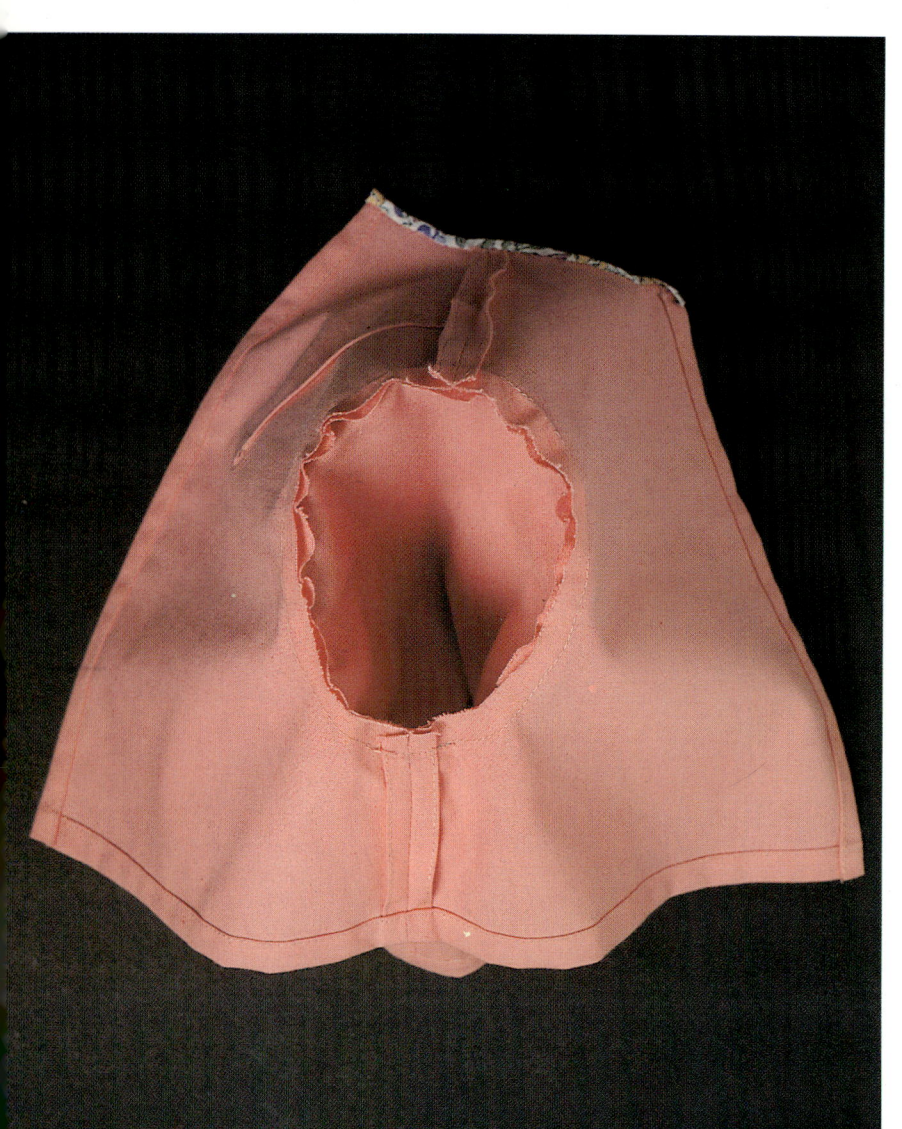

Setting in a zip (page 42)

Set-in sleeve tacked and sewn in position (page 45)

Pleated skirt (page 59)

Gathered skirt with Liberty print border and sash (page 56)

Pinafore (page 62)

Party frock (page 65)

Board shorts (page 68)

6. Pin cuff to sleeve, matching nicks, right sides together. Tack in place and machine. Remove tacking, trim seam edge.

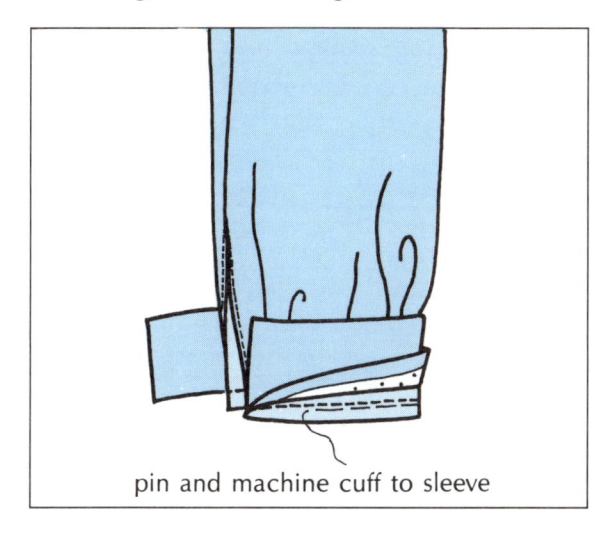

pin and machine cuff to sleeve

7. Press seam allowance towards cuff. Bring folded edge of sleeve facing to stitching line on wrong side of sleeve.
8. Pin and tack. Machine topstitch in place close to the edge.

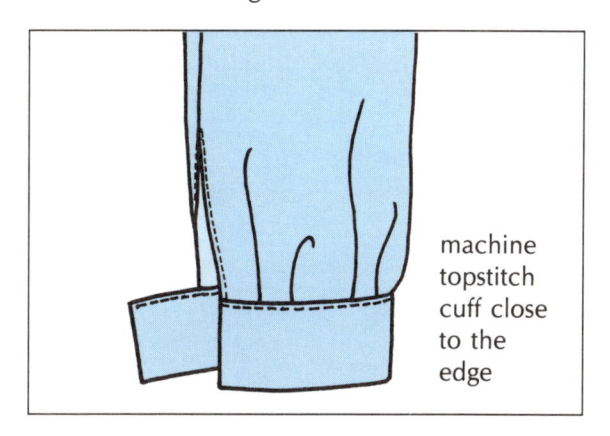

machine topstitch cuff close to the edge

9. Remove tacking and press cuff, holding a shoulder pad underneath to prevent creasing.

Waistband *(illustrated on page 36)*

Check that the waistband pattern is the right length for your waist measurement. Allow a little extra in the length, if need be, for tucking in a blouse and for comfort.

1. A waistband is best cut on the length of the material. This gives the least amount of stretch and is stronger.
2. Cut a strip of iron-on interfacing half the width of the waistband pattern. Cut off seam allowance to prevent bulkiness.
3. Press the interfacing onto the wrong side of the material (Fig.A).
4. Fold the band in half with right sides together.
5. At the right-hand edge, stitch down 4 cm, then 4 cm across to make the buttonhole section. Cut away excess fabric under this area. Trim the seam and cut seam corners on an angle to remove the bulk (Fig.B).

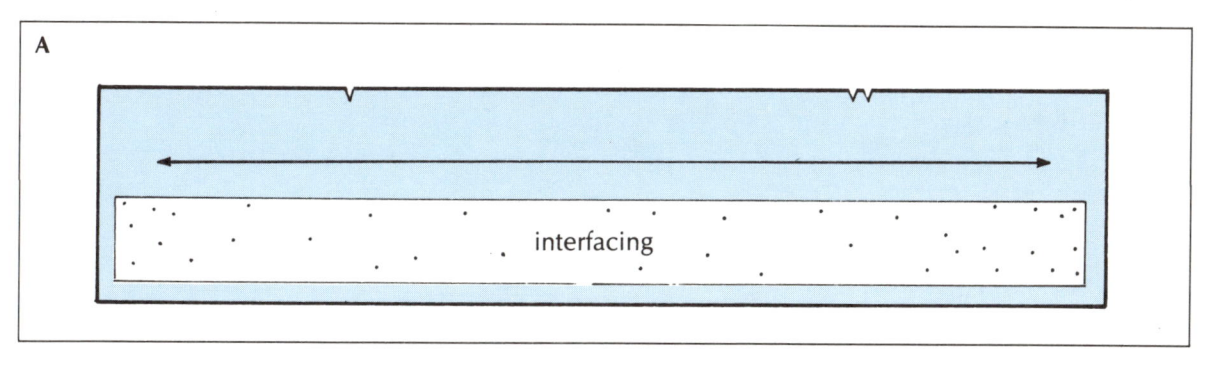

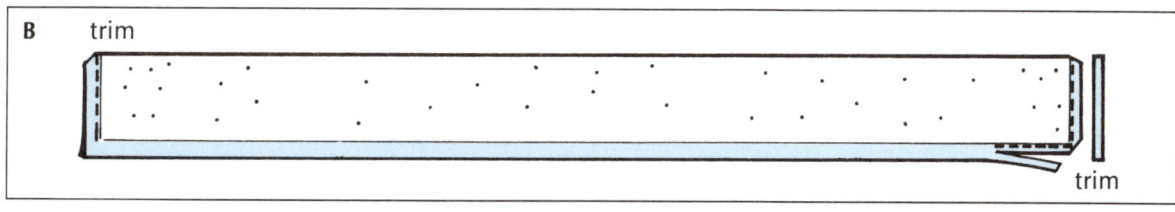

A

interfacing

B trim

trim

6. At the left-hand end sew a 1.5 cm seam.
7. Turn the waistband to the right side and press flat.
8. When joining the waistband to the skirt, turn skirt inside out and pin the right side of the waistband to the wrong side of the skirt.
9. Tack in place and machine. Trim away any bulk. Press the seam up towards the waistband.
10. Flip the waistband up and over the seam allowance to the right side of the garment.
11. Press the seam allowance and pin all along the edge of the waistband with the pins placed vertically (this prevents puckering).
12. Tack in place a little above the edge (Fig.C).
13. Machine close to the edge. Remove the tacking.
14. Press the waistband flat.
15. Make a buttonhole in the overlap area or attach fasteners (Fig.D).

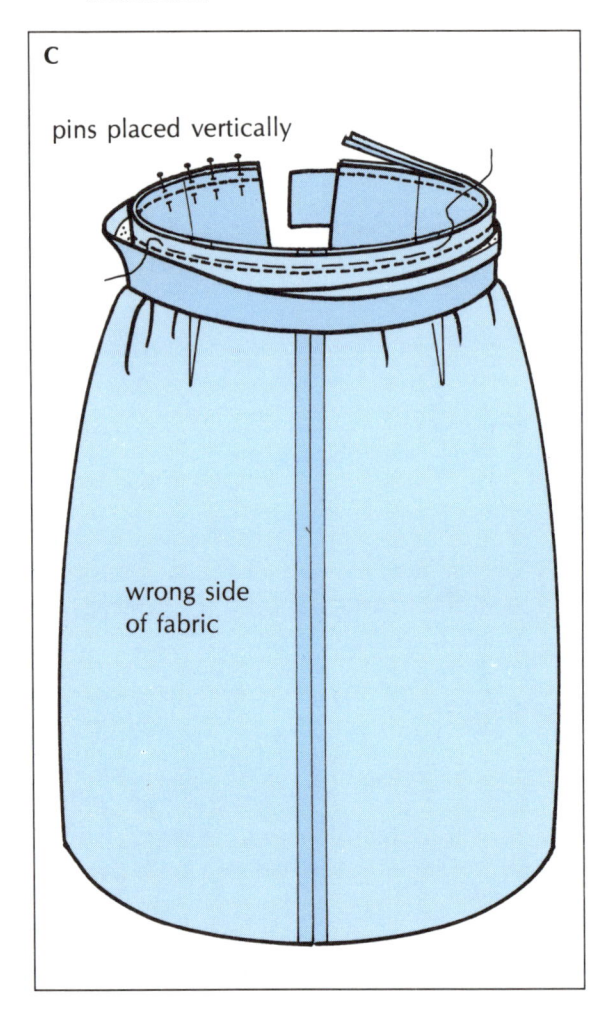

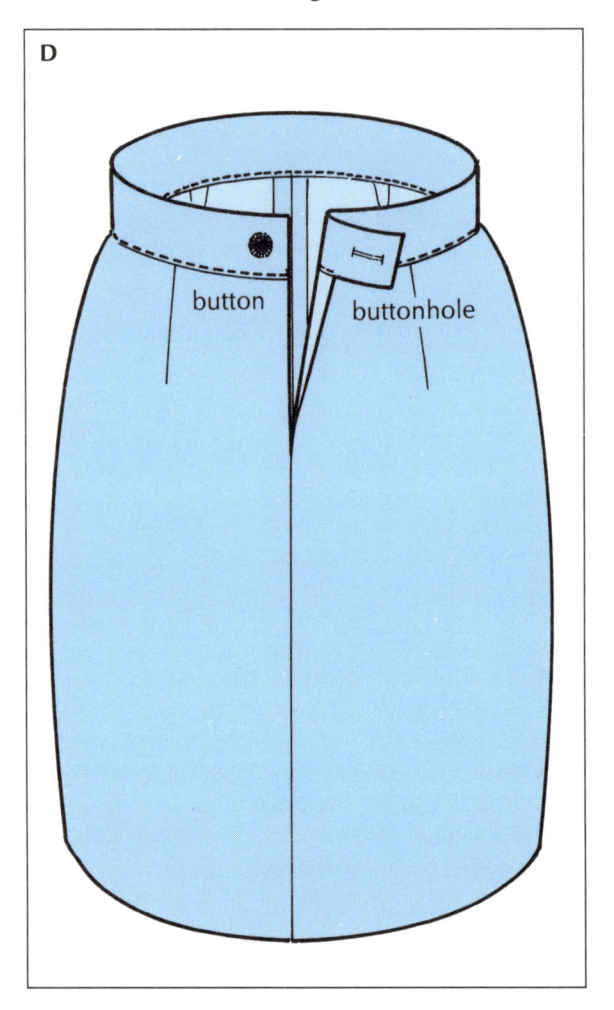

Setting in a zip *(illustrated on page 36)*

The lapped application method is used in skirts and frocks. Side zips are sewn in on the left, so the lap section is facing towards the back and you cannot look directly at the teeth. Use the zipper foot attachment on your machine to help you sew close to the zipper edge. Test the zip before you use it by pulling it up and down to make sure it runs freely. Remember, you must always tack a zip in place and the teeth should never be visible when wearing your garment.

Three points to remember:
- tack a zip in place
- use a zipper foot
- pull the head of the zip down out of the way until you pass that sewing area

1. Follow your pattern's instructions on how your zip seam area should be completed before setting in your zip (Fig.A).
2. Pull your zip up and down to test it is not faulty.
3. With the right side of the garment facing you, fold over each side of the top of the zip, hand stitch in place.
4. Still with the right side of the garment facing you, pin the closed zip from top to bottom next to the fold on the right hand side. On the other side (which now becomes the lap side) pin the zip 6 mm from the fold line from bottom to top.
5. Tack the zip in place to prevent it from moving, sewing bigger tacking stitches at the back (they are easier to remove). Use the same colour thread as your garment. The little tacking stitches, which are now visible on the right side, will help as a guide to sew straight (Fig.B).

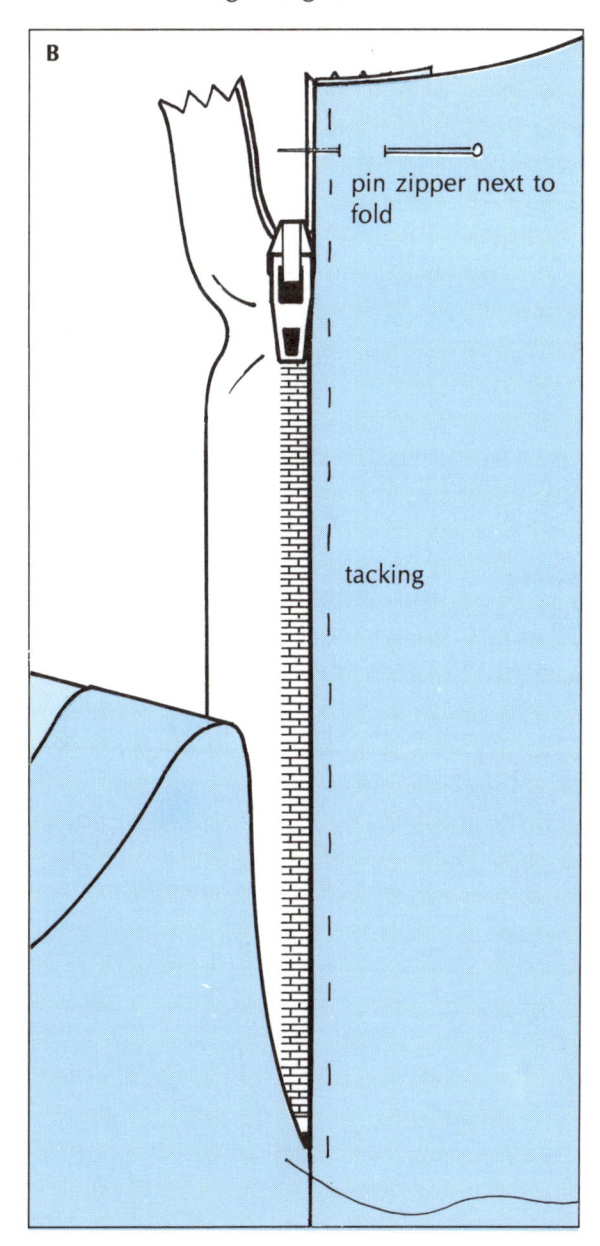

6. Put zipper foot in position on your machine. Check that there is enough thread in the bobbin to complete the sewing of this section of the zip in one step.
7. Start machining from the top of the lap side. First, pull the zip down 2 cm and sew this section. Lift the pressure foot, pull the zipper head back up and lower the foot, and then continue sewing down to the bottom of the zip. (Fig.C)
8. Pivot the fabric to sew across the bottom of the zip. Pivot again before going up the other side.
9. Continue sewing up towards the top. Stop 2 cm away from the top and pull the zipper head down and out of the way before sewing up to the top.
10. Remove tacking from the back, cutting threads out (Fig.D).
11. Stitch a hook at the top of the zip on the flap side, a little back from the edge. Sewing with a double thread and a knot, again a little back from the edge, make a double loop the size of the hook and blanket-stitch along its length. The hook and eye should not be visible when the person is wearing the garment.
12. Place a cloth over the zip and press lightly.

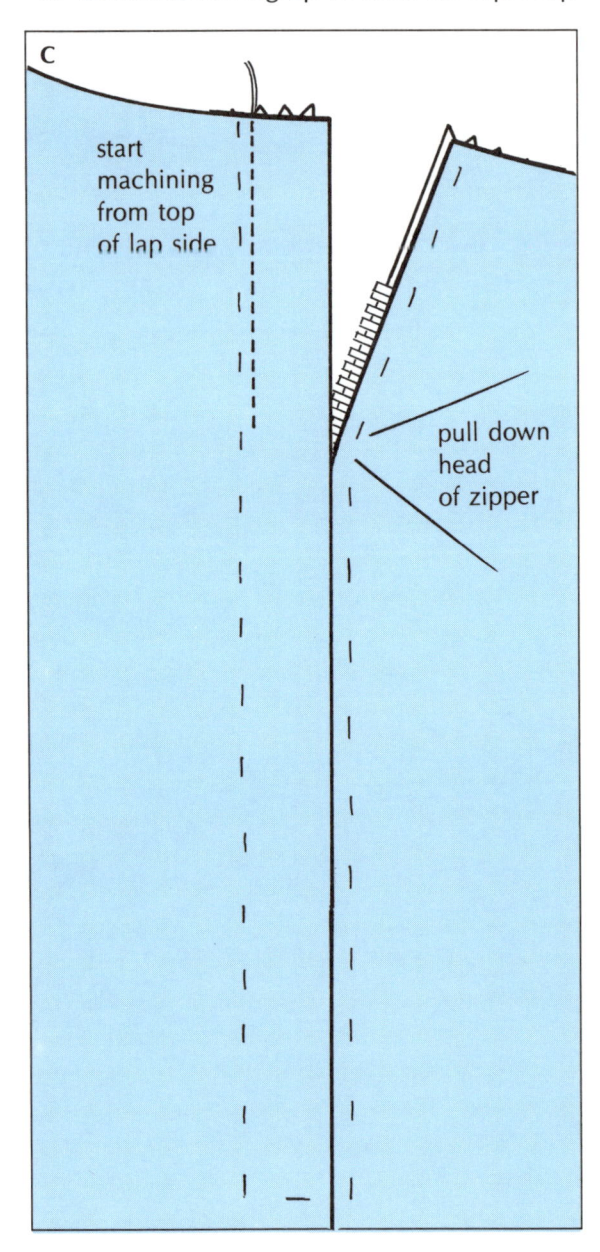

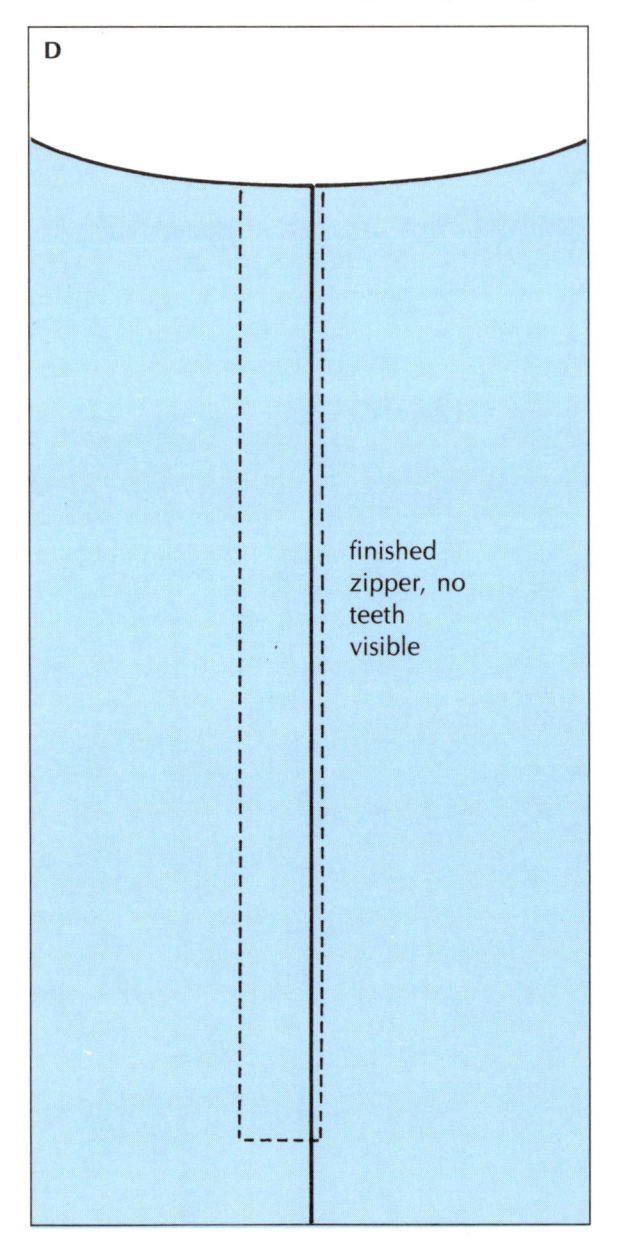

C

start machining from top of lap side

pull down head of zipper

D

finished zipper, no teeth visible

44

Sleeves

Set-in sleeve

(illustrated on page 36)

A set-in sleeve is a very tailored sleeve moulded into the armhole with no gathers. The sleeve pattern will have one notch at the front of the sleeve and two notches at the back. The back of the sleeve has extra measurement to allow for the movement of the body.

1. Using the largest stitch on your machine, sew a gathering row on the seam line at the top of the sleeve, starting at the front notch and going around to the two back notches.

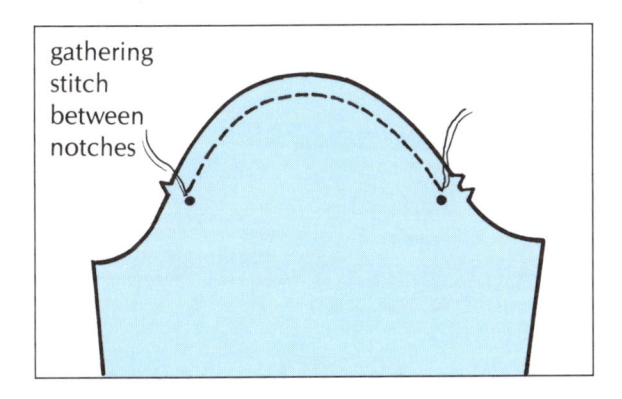

2. Stitch the underarm seam, neaten and press flat open.

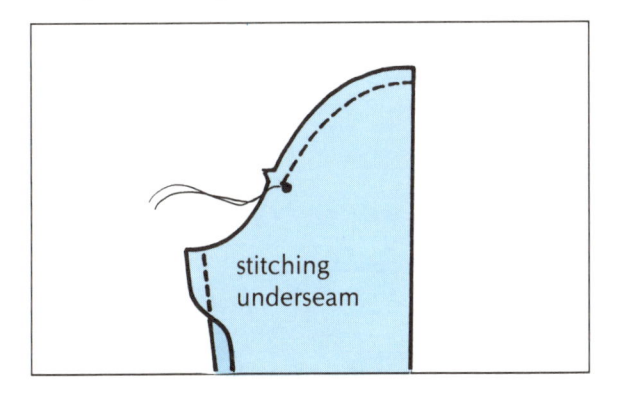

3. Turn the sleeve to the right side.
4. Hold the garment so you are looking into the armhole. Drop the sleeve into the armhole, right sides facing each other.
5. Match the seam lines and notches together. Pin top of sleeve to the shoulder seam, underarm seam to underarm seam, notches to notches. The area between the notches is where you ease in the sleeve.

Because the sleeve is slightly larger than the armhole at this stage, use the gathering thread to slightly ease the material to fit neatly into the armhole. The gathering thread is only to mould the sleeve head in place. There should be no puckering.

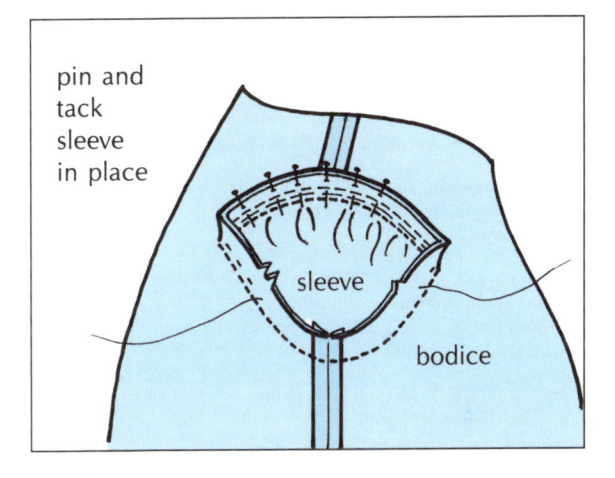

6. Tack in place all around the armhole.
7. Machine a little below the tacking, then remove the tacking, being careful not to stretch the armhole.
8. Sew a second row of stitching 6 mm away from sewing line, within the seam allowance.
9. Trim any bulk away.

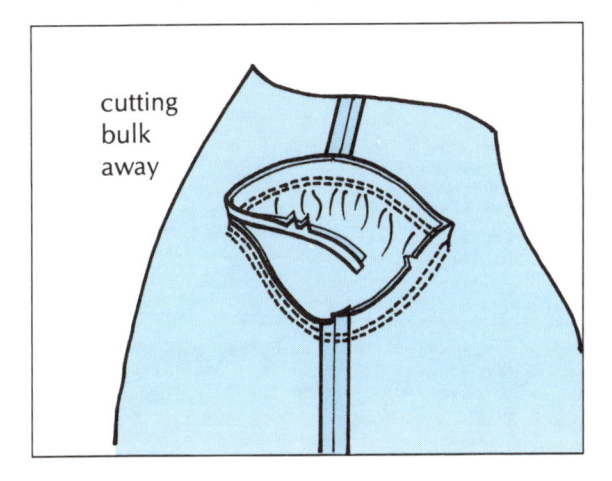

10. Press armhole seam (holding shoulder pad underneath) down towards the bottom of sleeve.

Shirt sleeve

Shirt sleeves have no gather as they have a much lower sleeve cap curve. A shirt sleeve is sewn to the body of the garment before the side seams are sewn together. The same method is used for a garment with dropped shoulders.

1. On the top of the sleeve seam allowance, run a gathering stitch by machine between the front armhole notch and the two back notches.
2. With right sides together, pin the sleeve to the armhole edge of the bodice, matching all notches.
3. Use the gathering thread to ease the sleeve in the area between the nicks, the same way as for the set-in sleeve. Make sure you have no folds; the easing is only to mould the sleeve into place in the armhole.
4. Tack, then machine stitch in place all around the armhole section. Remove tacking. 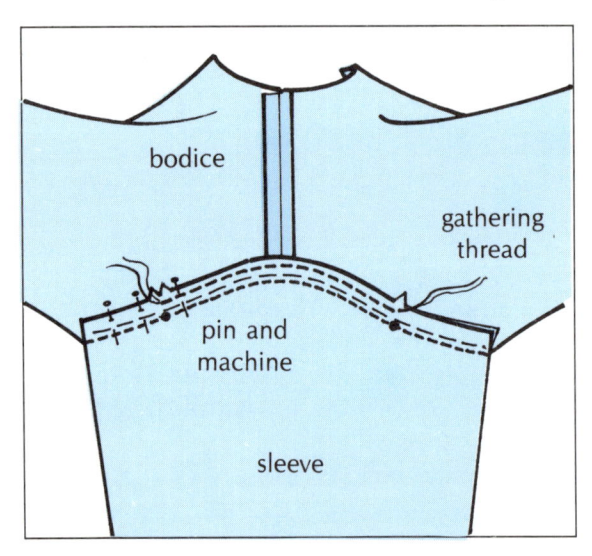 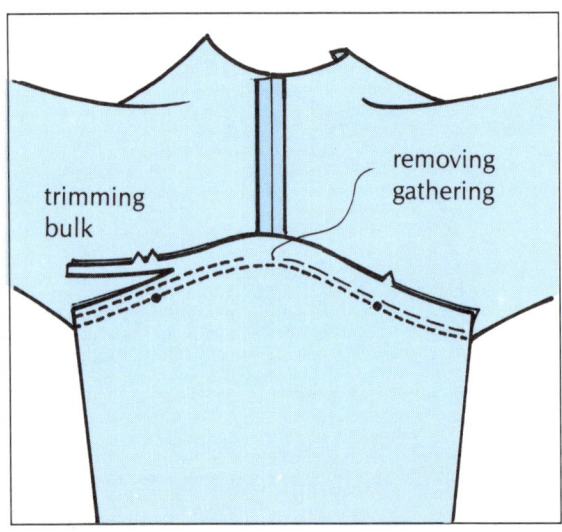
5. Neaten the seam, cut any bulk away. Machine another row of stitching in the same allowance, 6 mm from the sleeve stitching.
6. Press seam down towards bottom of garment.
7. Pin, tack and machine the side seams of the garment; neaten edges. Press seam towards the back.

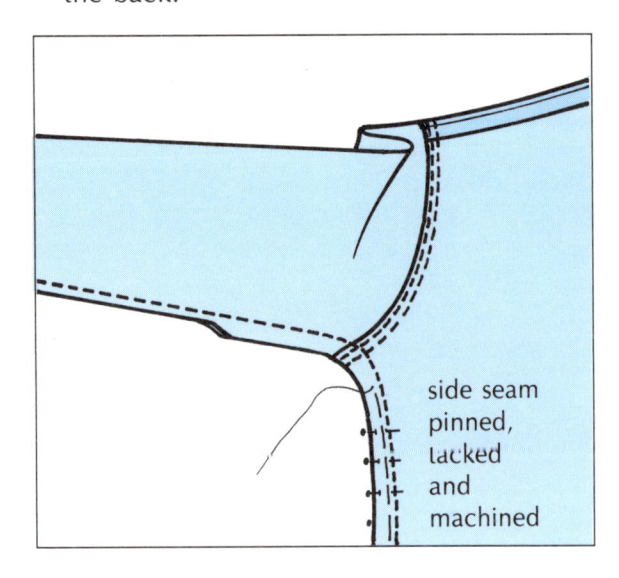

Raglan sleeve

The raglan sleeve is sewn to the garment in one continuous seam which runs from the neckline to the underarm. If a shoulder dart is marked on the pattern it will help the sleeve to fit and hang correctly.

1. Mark dart position (if any) with tailor's chalk. Pin and tack in place. Machine from top to bottom of dart. Tie thread ends and remove tacking.

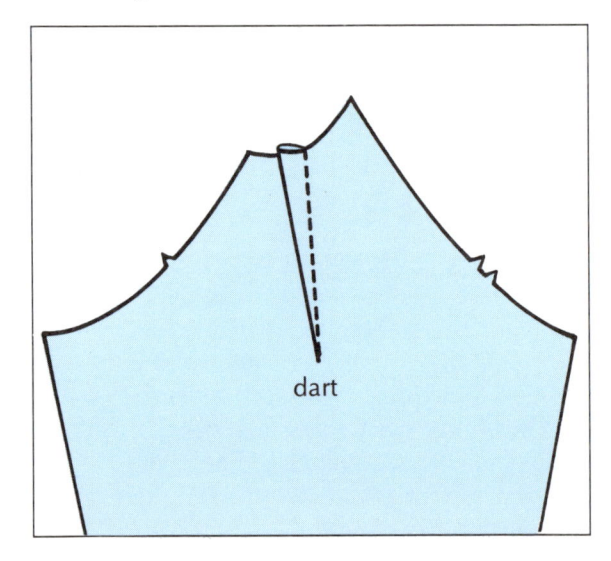

2. Press dart flat, then cut through centre nearly to the end of the dart to help it lie flat.

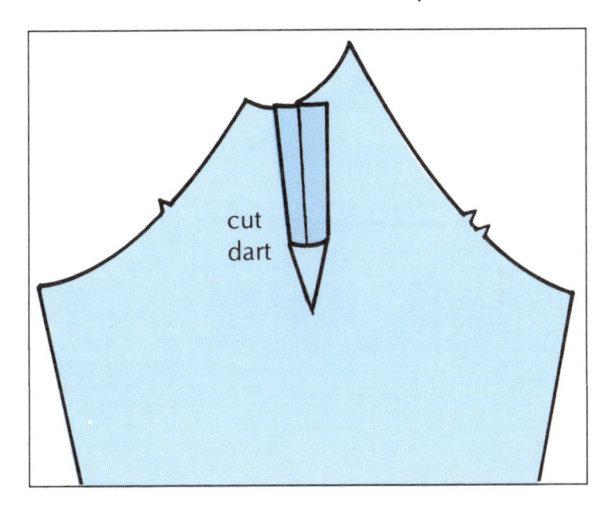

3. From the top of the sleeves, pin the diagonal seams of the sleeve to the bodice with right sides together, matching the notches.
4. Tack in place and machine. Remove tacking.

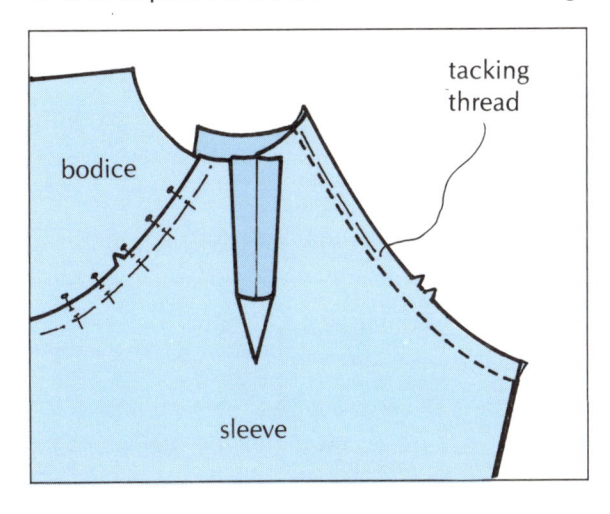

5. Trim seam and cut small nicks evenly spaced about 25 mm along edge of seam. Press seam open.

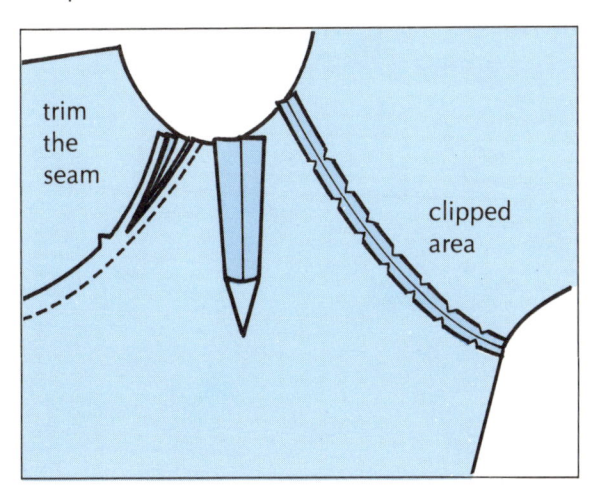

6. Pin the side seams of the garment, from the end of the sleeve down to the waistline. Machine.
7. Cut nicks 25 mm apart in curved area of the underarm. Neaten edges and press seam flat towards the back.

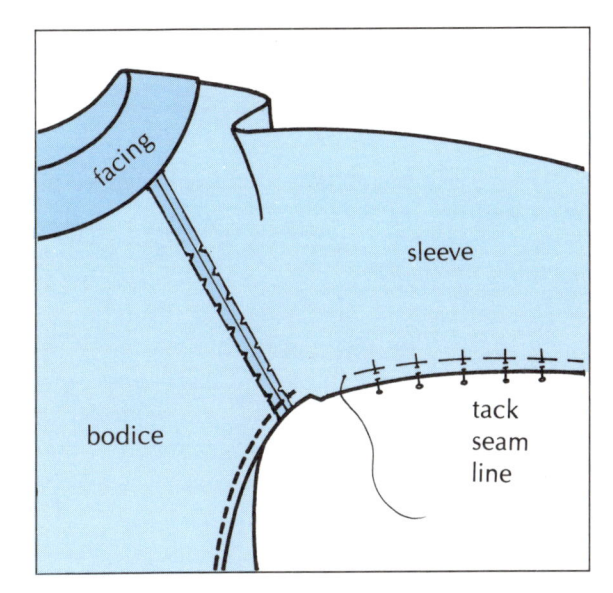

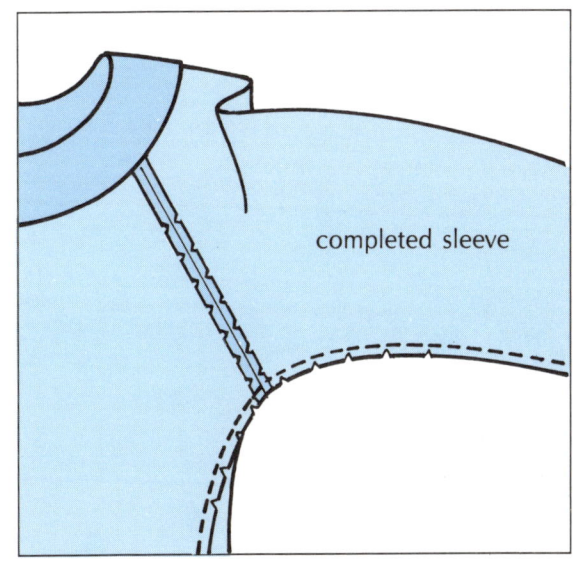

Pockets

Pockets are not only functional, but in different shapes and sizes can be another feature trim. They are sewn on the garment while it is flat open, before side seams are sewn together.

1. Always follow the pattern guide instructions carefully.
2. Make sure that pairs of pockets are the same shape and size.
3. The pattern will indicate a placement line to be marked on the garment.
4. Always pin and baste pockets onto the garment to keep them absolutely straight.
5. Trim away any bulk and press well at each step.

Patch pockets

1. Use tailor's chalk to mark the pocket placement line on the garment.

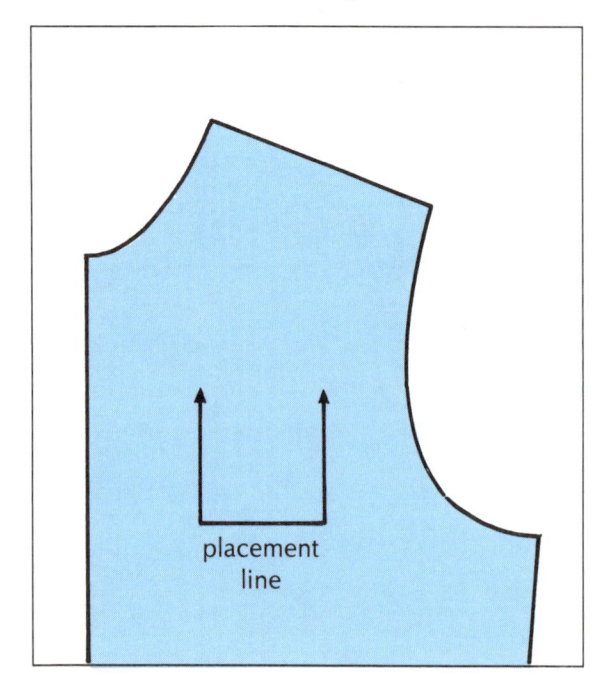

2. Press top edge of pocket under 6 mm.

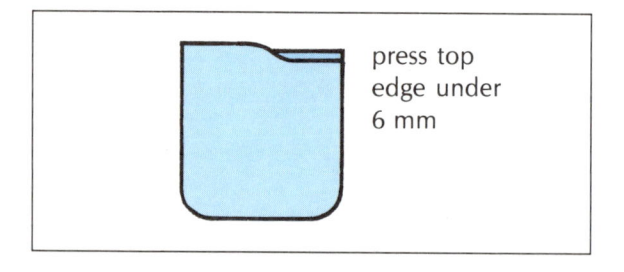

3. Turn top of pocket to outside on hemline. Starting at hem fold, stitch around raw edges at 15 mm.

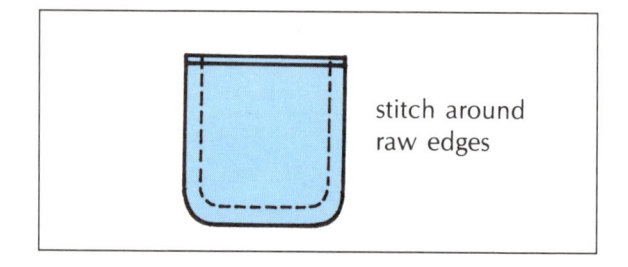

4. Cut corners diagonally to remove bulk.

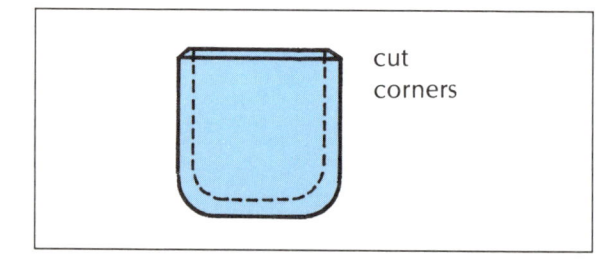

5. Turn hem to inside. Press under seam allowance below hem on line of stitching.
6. Machine hem in place.

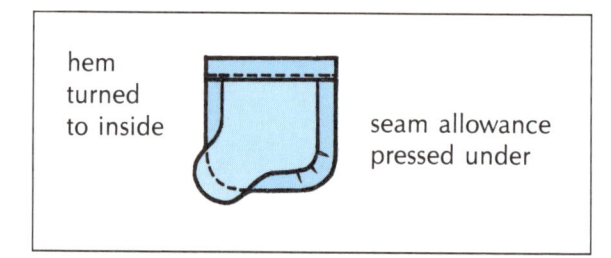

7. Pin pocket on placement line and baste to keep pocket on grainline.

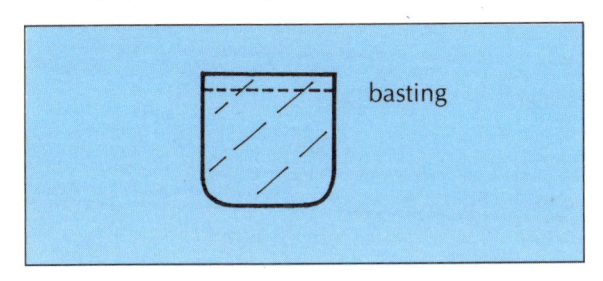

basting

8. Machine in place close to the edge and press flat.

9. If the pocket has a button and buttonhole, the buttonhole is sewn before stitching pocket to the garment. The button is sewn in place last.

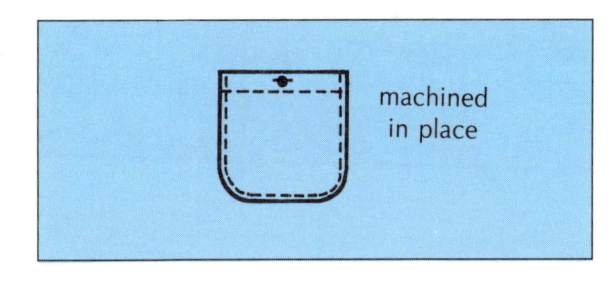

machined in place

Pleats

Pleats control fullness and give a lot of body comfort to the wearer. The style of pleating you choose will depend on the pattern requirements, the choice of fabric and your figure.

Knife pleats

Knife pleats hang in a very soft line. They all run in the same direction. They can be pressed from the waistline down to the second hip measurement, or be pressed all the way to the hemline.

Box pleats (on right)

Box pleats are a traditional style of pleating. They were nearly always used in school uniforms until quite recently. The two folds of each pleat are turned away from each other.

Inverted pleats

Inverted pleats are two folds that meet evenly at the centre of the waist and face each other. The line of a skirt with inverted pleats can be very slimming, as the hip area has no pleats.

Hand-sewing

Any hand-sewing for the finished stages of a garment must be very neat. Use fine sewing needles and the correct matching cotton. The less hand-sewing there is the more professional the finished garment will look.

Hemstitching

Hemstitching is an invisible stitch suitable for hems and sleeve edges, particularly on sheer and silk fabrics to help the garment hang properly and have a professional finish.

1. Level the hemline carefully and press raw edge up 13 mm to the wrong side. Machine stitch close to the edge.
2. Turn up the hem allowance placing the pins vertically all around the hemline.
3. Thread a fine sewing needle with matching cotton, make a tiny knot at the end.
4. Start from right to left at the seam line and fasten the knot in place under the fold. Picking up hardly any threads of the garment, pull thread through and run the needle along the top of folded edge to form a stitch. Continue all the way around the hem.
5. Finish with a backstitch in the fold area. Press hem flat on wrong side with a press cloth.

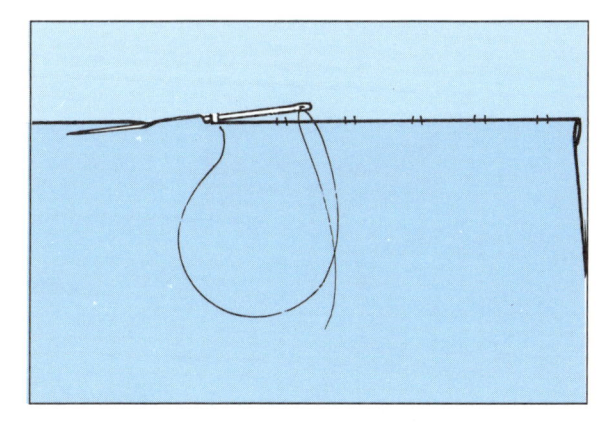

Slipstitching

Slipstitching is an almost invisible stitch which when properly done cannot be seen on the right side of the garment. When hemming a sheer or silk fabric, a slipped hem is advisable as it will help the fabric hang properly.

1. Level the hemline carefully. Press the raw edge up 13 mm to the wrong side. Machine stitch close to this edge.
2. Turn up the hem allowance, placing the pins vertically all around the hemline.
3. Thread a fine sewing needle with matching cotton and make a tiny knot at the end.
4. Starting from right to left at the seamline, fasten the knot in place under the fold. Picking up hardly any threads of the fabric, pull the thread through and then through a few threads of the fold edge. Continue in this way all around the hem.
5. Finish the hem with a back stitch in the fold area.
6. Press the hem flat on the wrong side.

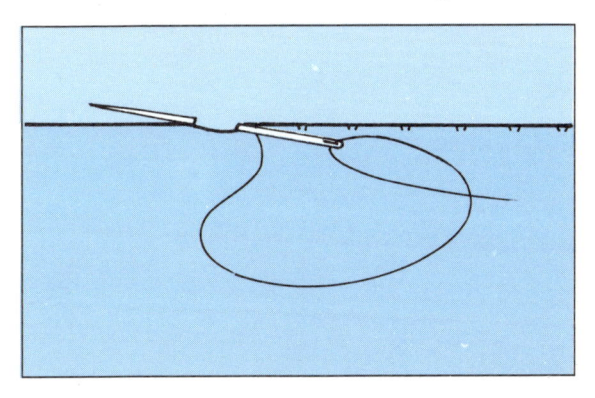

Buttonholes

Machine buttonholes

Buttonholes can easily be made with a sewing machine if you have a buttonhole foot. Follow the guide in your sewing machine manual. Practise on as many types and thicknesses of fabric as you can. Remember to adjust the tension on your machine when you are sewing thick fabrics. Keep practising until your buttonholes look professional. The rule is that buttonholes are sewn on right side over left for women's clothes and left side over right for men's clothes.

Hand-sewn buttonholes

1. Measure the width of the button before you mark the size of the buttonhole. Buttons are not completely flat, so you must allow for the 'rise'.
2. On the right side of the garment mark the position of the buttonhole and its length.

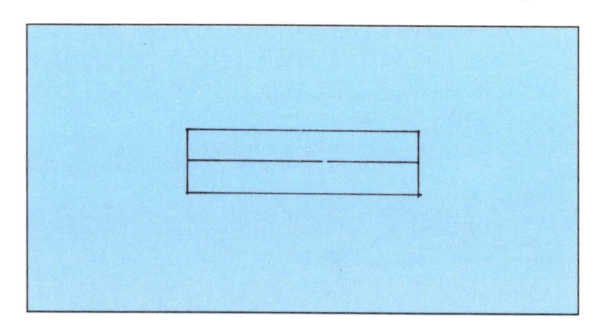

3. Using only the point of your scissors, cut through all thicknesses of fabric between the end markings. Insert the point of the scissors at the centre and cut to one end, then cut to the other end.

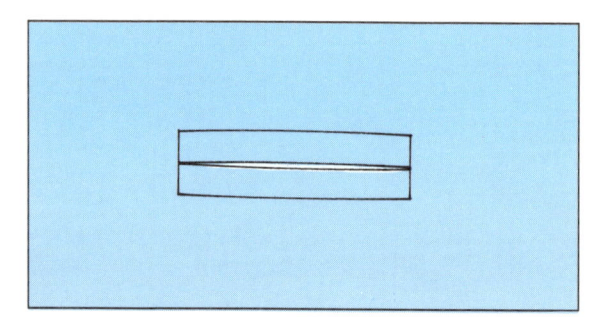

4. Using thread to match the fabric, thread a needle with double thread, with a small knot at the end. Allow enough length for the complete buttonhole.
5. Secure the thread underneath the slit at the top. Bring the thread to the front from right to left under the point of the needle and draw through the loop so that the little knot comes at the edge of the slit. Continue this buttonhole stitch along one cut edge, and then along the other.

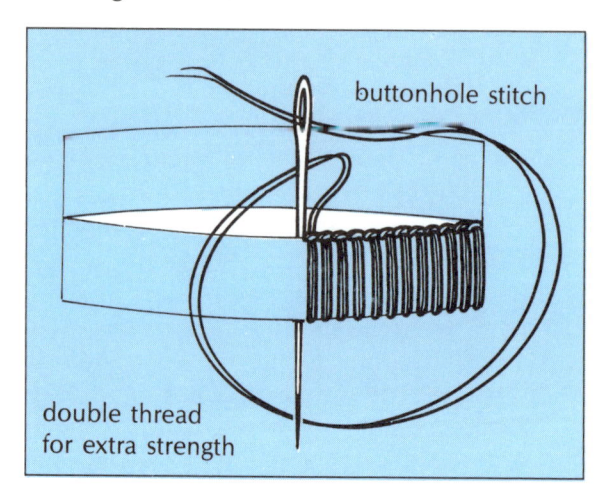

6. At each end of the buttonhole sew a bar of horizontal stitches to reinforce and complete the buttonhole.

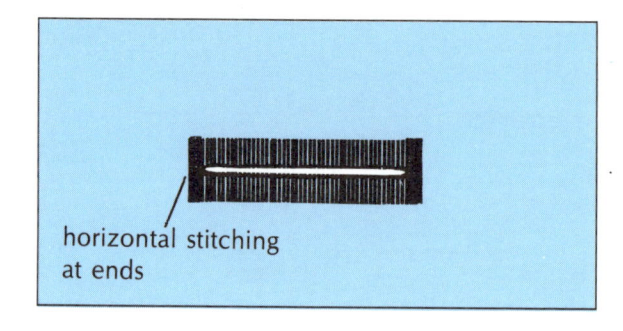

Sewing on buttons

As well as being functional, buttons can give a very smart finish to a garment. On a very tailored garment, for example, buttons properly selected can give a finish as smart as adding jewellery or accessories.

Sew-through buttons

1. Pattern guides often contain a specially marked strip which can be pinned to your garment to give you the correct placement for the button. Remember, buttons go left under right for women's clothes, right under left for men's (this matches the buttonholes).

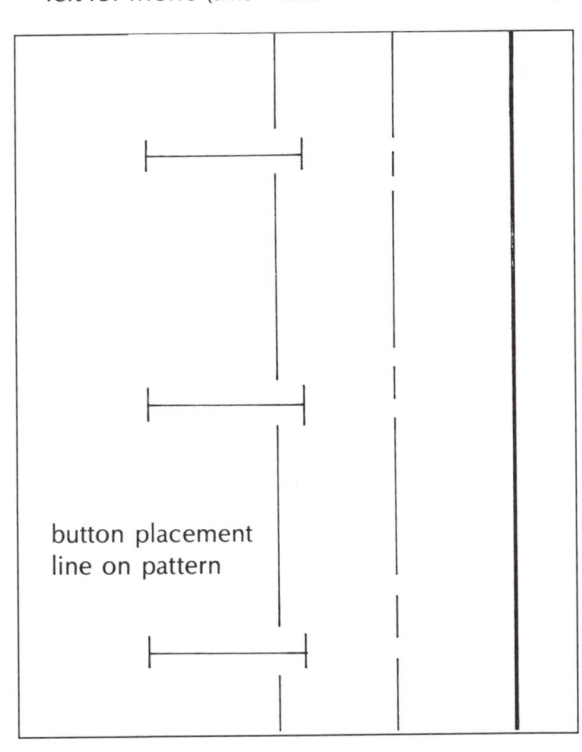

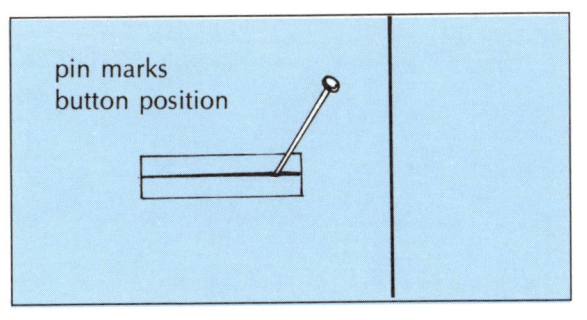

2. Place a pin right through the centre of the buttonhole. Using a double thread and a knot, make a back stitch on the pin mark.
3. Stitch the button in place, sewing in and out through the holes at least four times.
4. Reinforce the strength of the stitching by winding the thread around the stitches, underneath the button. This makes a 'shank' and raises the button a little from the fabric. Backstitch to secure the thread and cut close to the garment.

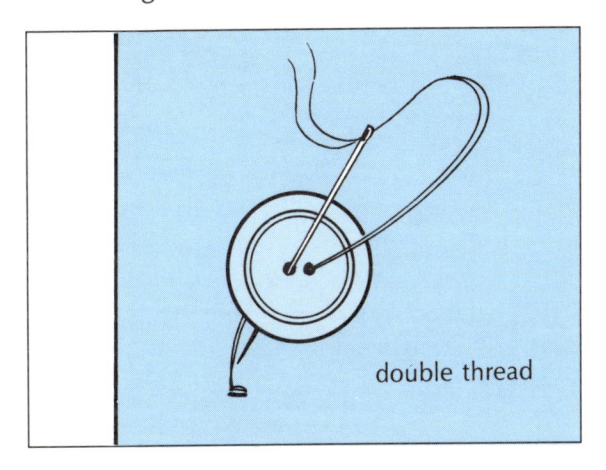

Shank buttons

Shank buttons have a ring at the back of the button. They are essential on garments like woollen overcoats, men's waistcoats and blazers. Covered buttons have a back ring as well—they are often designed to be used on the backs of wedding gowns, where a zip is eliminated. They can also be used on the wrist opening of long classical sleeves.

1. Mark the position for the button on the right side of the garment.
2. Remember, as for sew-through buttons, it is left under right for women's clothes and right under left for men's.
3. With a strong double thread and a knot, make a backstitch where the button is to be sewn. Space the thread a little way from the ring.

4. Stitch in and out the ring at least four times to secure. Wind the thread from the ring down to the garment. (This extra 'length' for the shank is essential when working with heavy woollen fabrics and other thick fabrics.) Backstitch to secure thread and cut close to the garment.

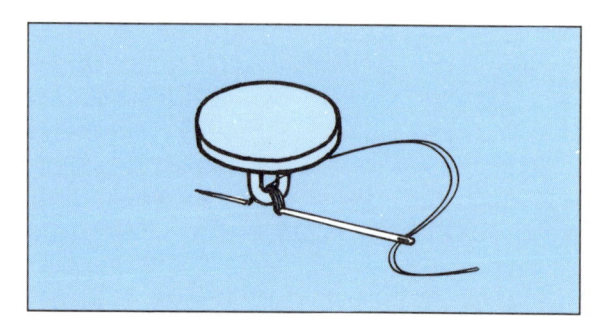

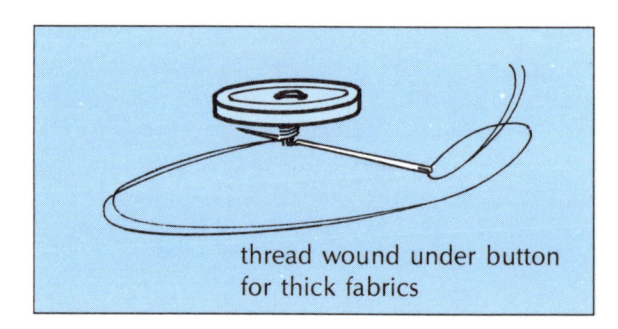

thread wound under button for thick fabrics

Hooks and eyes

Hooks and eyes are used where two edges need to be held together. They come in a variety of sizes. A larger size is best used on waistlines where there is extra strain on the garment. Loop eyes and straight eyes are available.

Edges that meet

A neater finish for a neckline closing is obtained by making your own 'eye' from thread, 'buttonholing' along a doubled length of thread in the required position. The hook and eye should never be visible when joined.

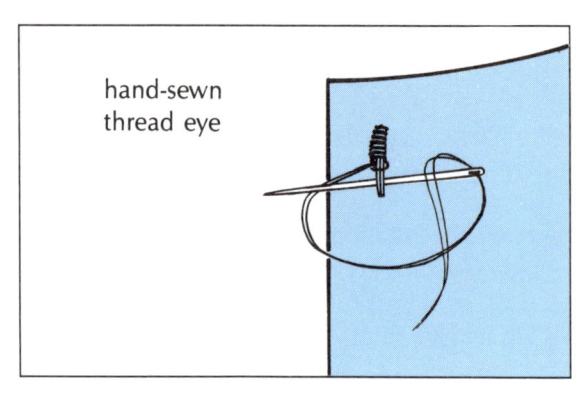

hand-sewn thread eye

Overlapping edges

1. On a waistband, for example, place the hook on the inside of the overlap about 6 mm in from the edge.
2. Stitch around each 'hole' with a buttonhole stitch.
3. Pass the needle through the middle of the hook, then stitch over it three or four times to hold it flat against the fabric.
4. Mark position of the eye on the other side of the garment, placing a pin where the end of the hook falls.
5. Stitch a straight eye in place with a buttonhole stitch around each hole.

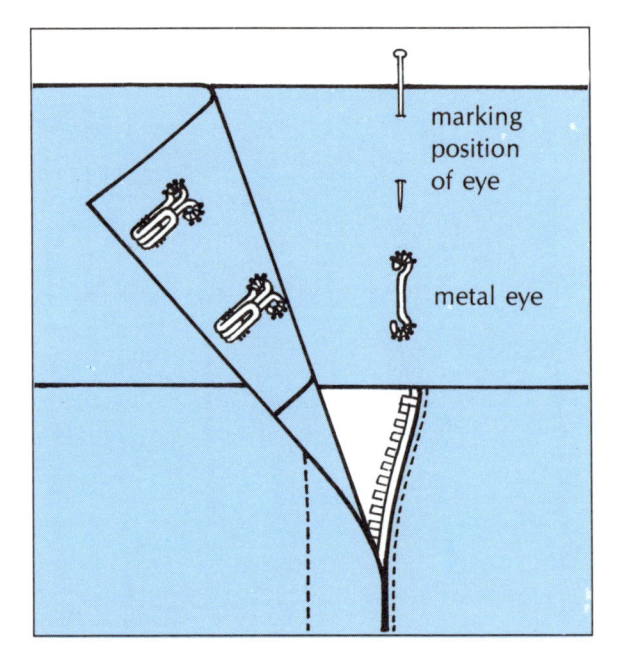

marking position of eye

metal eye

Patterns

Gathered skirt with Liberty print border and sash

(illustrated on page 37)

This skirt is easy to sew. With its cottage print border and matching sash it is a very pretty garment to start a summer wardrobe.

Materials required:

- 90 cm wide fabric, twice the length of skirt, plus seam allowances
- Liberty or cottage print fabric for skirt border and sash
- Drafting paper (3 metres)
- Non-roll elastic (2 cm wide); enough for waist, plus joining overlap
- Thread (check Needle and Thread Chart, page 12)

Measurements:

1. Length of skirt from waist to hem, plus hem allowance
2. Waist
3. Width of skirt (same as fabric)
4. Length and width of sash (sash is 23 cm deep, and at least 3 times longer than waist measurement)

Drafting pattern

Skirt

1. Draw a straight line on the left-hand side of your paper the length of the skirt, plus 90 mm for seams (mark A). Write *Foldline* on the line.
2. Square lines from top and bottom of line A. Mark them B and C.
3. Join B and C (call this line D).
4. From top of line B measure down 75 mm, draw a line across (mark it E). This is the fold for elastic casing. Write *Opening* on line.
5. Measure up border distance from bottom of C and rule across (mark this line F).
6. Draw a vertical line on the pattern to mark lengthwise grainline.
7. Write *Front and Back, Cut 2.*

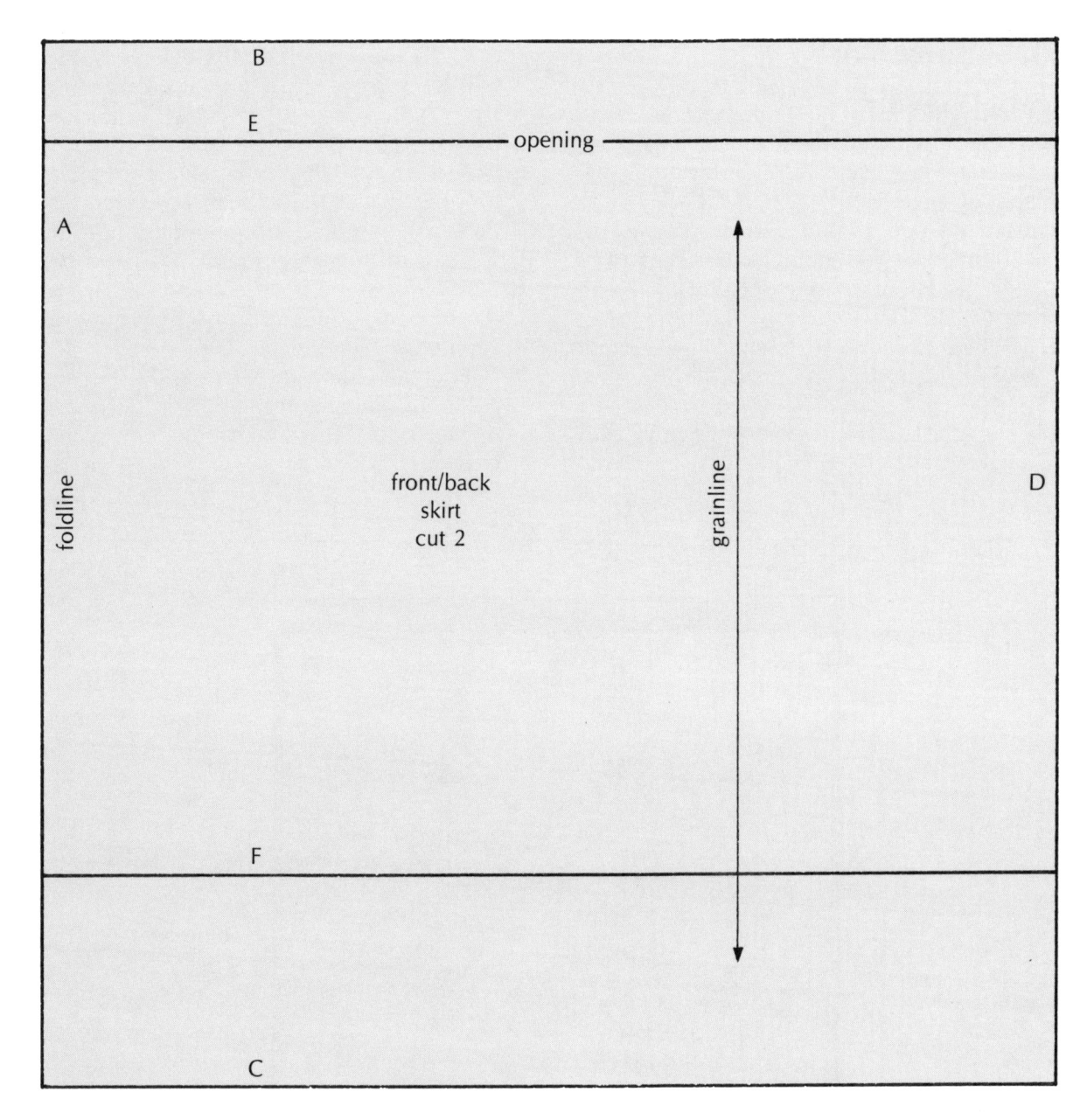

Sash

1. On left hand side of paper draw a straight line the width of the sash, 23 cm (mark A). Write *Foldline*.
2. The sash needs to be at least three times the waist measurement in length. Halve this measurement and draw lines across from the top and bottom of line A (mark them B and C). Join B and C.
3. Write *Sash, Cut 2,* on fold.

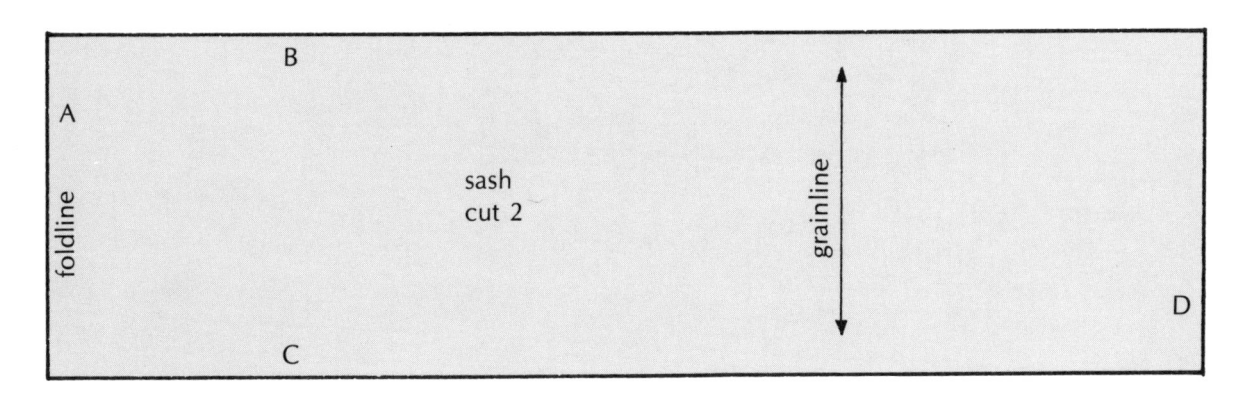

Machining skirt

1. With right sides of front and back together, pin, tack and machine side seams. Remove tacking. Press seams together towards back and zig-zag edges.
2. From the top 13 mm fold, turn down to 75 mm on the wrong side (to line E), pin and tack, leaving a 25 mm opening to thread elastic.
3. Machine casing close to edge. Sew another row of stitching 25 mm from the top. Turn skirt to right side.
4. Cut elastic to fit your waist comfortably, plus an allowance for joining. Pin a safety pin to one end and ease elastic through the casing. Join lap together. Machine along opening.
5. From bottom of skirt, press a 15 mm fold towards the top on right side of fabric.
6. Cut strips of Liberty or cottage print fabric to fit width of skirt. Join seams and press flat.
7. Press a 15 mm fold top and bottom on the wrong side of border fabric.
8. Pin border to the bottom of the skirt and at the top edge. Tack and machine close to each edge. Remove tacking.
9. Cut out sash, join right sides together, leaving a 75 mm opening in the middle. Turn sash right side out. Press, and hand-stitch opening closed.

Front/back skirts machined at side seams. Elastic casing with opening

Blocks of cottage print fabric make border

Pleated skirt *(illustrated on page 37)*

The skirt is made of a knife-pleated section joined to a yoke with an elastic waist. It can be teamed with jumpers or blouses. It is very comfortable to wear, as well as looking smart and modern.

Materials required:

- The amount of 115 cm wide fabric required will be twice the length of the skirt plus seam allowances
- Matching colour thread
- Non-roll elastic (2.5 cm wide) for waist, plus extra for join

Measurements:

1. Waist
2. Width of hip
3. Length of yoke (from waist to hip)
4. Length of skirt from hip to hem

Drafting the pattern

Skirt yoke

Use drafting paper 46 cm square.

1. Mark left-hand side of paper Line A, write *Fold line*.
2. Mark top of paper Line B.
3. Mark right-hand side of paper Line C.
4. Mark bottom of paper Line D.
5. Measure down line A from line B the depth of the measurement from waist to hipline plus 75 mm (for casing for elastic), plus 15 mm for seam line. Mark this point E.
6. Along line B from line A measure half hip measurement plus 15 mm for seamline. Mark this point F.
7. Draw a line across the paper from point E and another line down the paper from point F. Where the lines cross, mark point G. These are the cutting lines.
8. Draw broken lines 15 mm inside the pattern and parallel to lines EG and FG. These are seam lines.
9. Mark a point 75 mm down line A from line B and draw a line across the paper to meet the side seam line. This is the elastic casing.

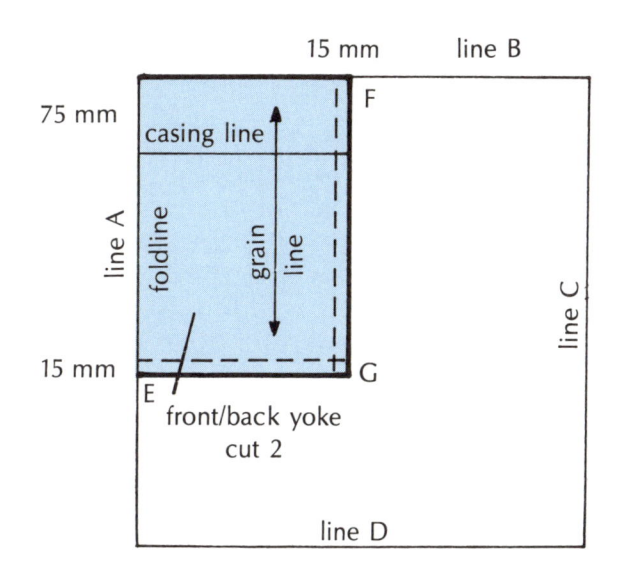

front/back yoke cut 2

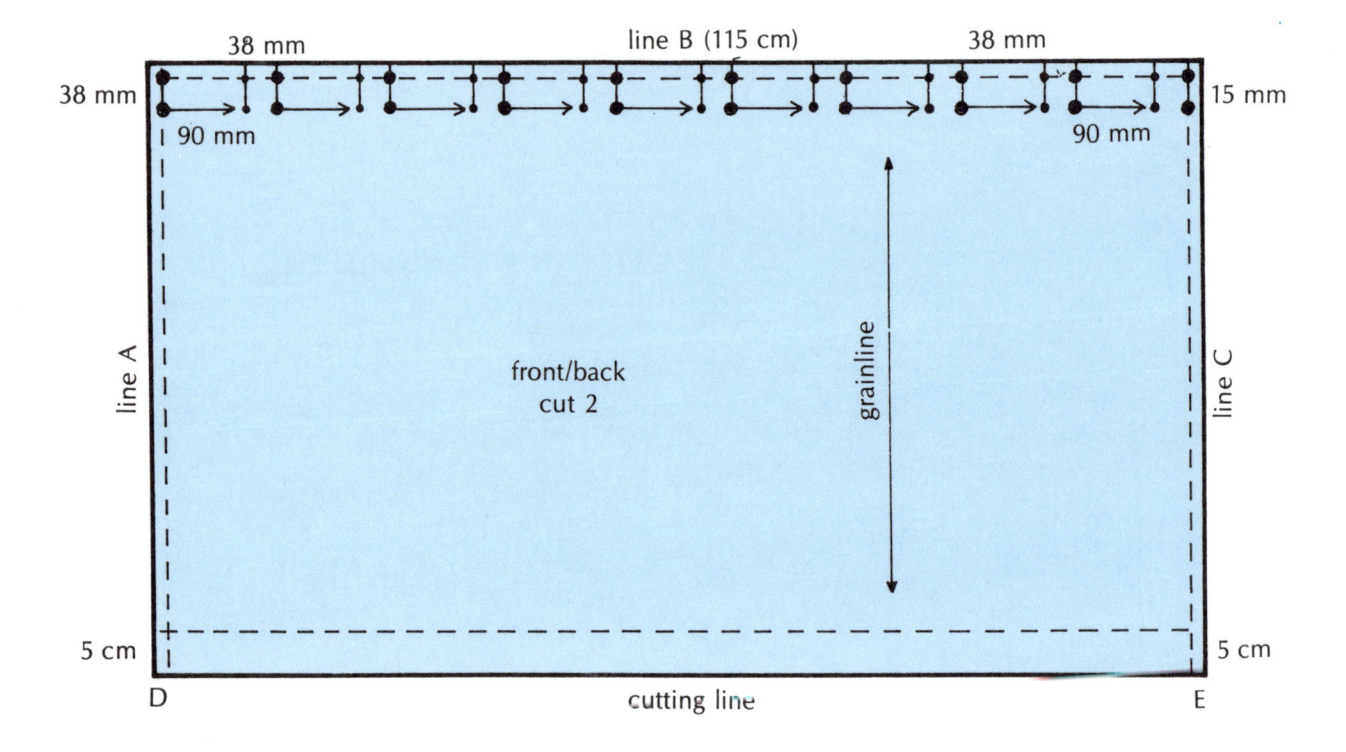

10. Write *Front/Back Yoke, Cut 2* on the pattern.
11. Draw a vertical line to mark lengthwise grainline.
12. Cut out pattern on cutting line.

Pleated skirt

Use drafting paper 115 cm wide and depth of length of skirt, plus 5 cm hem allowance.

1. Down left hand side of paper, write Line A (cutting line).
2. At top of paper, write Line B (cutting line).
3. Down right-hand side of paper, write Line C (cutting line).
4. Measure down line A from line B the depth of skirt plus 5 cm allowance; mark this point D.
5. Meausure down line C from line B the depth of skirt plus 5 cm allowance; mark this point E.
6. Joint point D to point E (cutting line).
7. Draw broken lines parallel and 15 mm inside the pattern from line A and line C. These are the side seam lines.
8. Draw a broken line parallel to line B and 15 mm inside the pattern. This is the waist seam line.
9. Along the waist seam line draw boxes 90 mm wide and 38 mm deep, and 38 mm apart (see diagram).
10. Mark top and bottom left-hand side of boxes with large circles.
11. Mark top and bottom right-hand side of boxes with small circles.
12. Mark a point 5 cm up line A from point D, and another 5 cm up line B from point E; join these wth a dotted line. This is the hemline.
13. Write *Front/Back, Cut 2* on the pattern.
14. Draw a vertical line to mark the lengthwise grainline.
15. Cut out pattern on cutting line.

Machining yoke

1. With right sides of front and back together, pin, tack and machine side seams. Remove tacking, press seams together towards the back, zig-zag edge of seams.
2. Fold down from the top to 75 mm on the wrong side and pin all the way around, leaving a 25 mm opening to thread elastic.

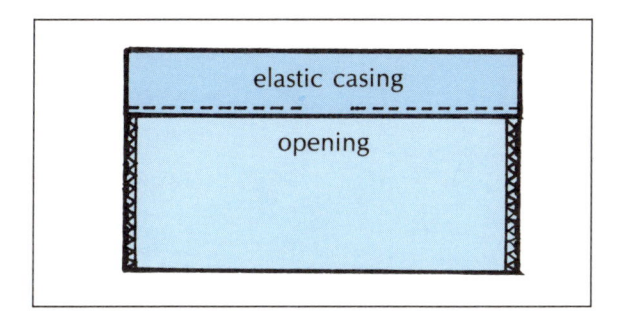

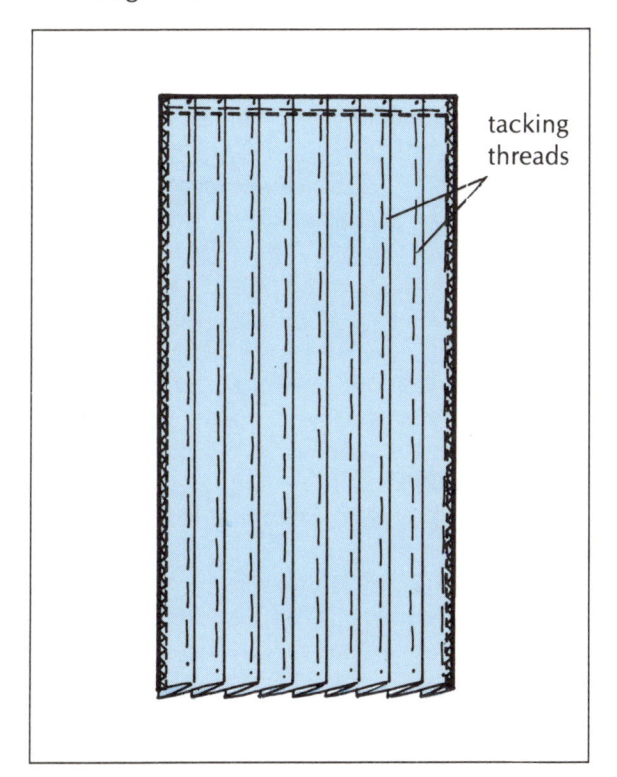

5. With right sides of yoke and skirt together, pin, matching centres and side seams. Tack and machine. Machine again 6 mm away from seam in seam allowance. Press seam towards the top.
6. Thread elastic with a safety pin through opening of casing to fit waist measurement. Stitch the lap in place. Machine across opening.
7. Press seam allowance on hem, pin in place. Slipstitch hem.
8. Using a pressing cloth, press pleats flat, remove tacking and press again.

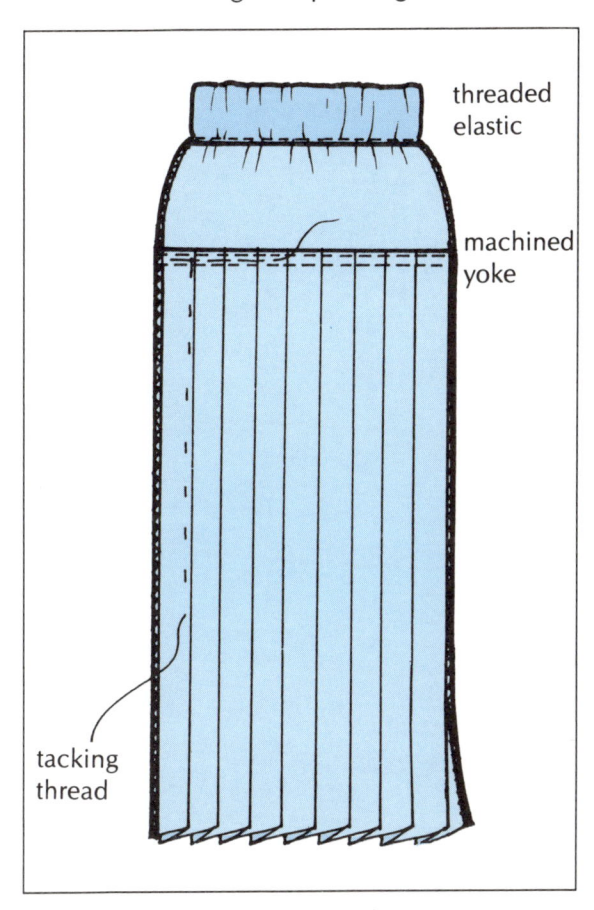

Pleating skirt

Before cutting skirt, transfer all pleat marks to the fabric by using double tailor's tacks in one colour for the large circles and single tailor's tacks in another colour for the small circles.

1. Join seams of skirt, neaten edges with zigzag stitch, turn skirt to right side.
2. Starting from one side seam, fold the fabric and bring a pair of double tailor's tacks to meet the next pair of single tailor's tacks. Pin in place.
3. Keep pleating until the skirt fits the bottom of the yoke. Tack pleats 15 mm down from the top and machine.
4. Tack each pleat in place down to the hem. This will help with the final pressing. Turn to wrong side.

Pinafore *(illustrated on page 38)*

This striped pinafore is a very comfortable garment to wear and an easy pattern to draft. It takes very little time to sew. The fabric is a stretch knit material.

Materials required:

- Drafting paper 75 cm square
- Stretch fabric 150 cm wide; twice the skirt length and twice the bodice lenth
- 100% polyester matching thread
- Ballpoint machine needle
- Motif for decoration

Measurements:

1. Length from shoulder to bottom of bodice
2. Depth of neckline (measure from centre throat to required depth, e.g. 10 cm)
3. Width of shoulder
4. Chest measurement
5. Waist measurement
6. Length from underarm to bottom of bodice
7. Length of skirt from waist to hem
8. Width of skirt, allowing for gathering (150 cm)

Drafting pattern

Bodice

1. Draw a 70 cm line down from top on left-hand side of paper. Mark it A and write *Foldline* on the line.
2. Square lines from top and bottom of line A 46 cm long (mark them B and C).
3. Join B and C (mark this line D).
4. From top of line A measure down to depth of neckline (point E).
5. Along line B measure half the width of the neck (point F).
6. From point F draw shoulder width sloping down 13 mm (point G).
7. From the top of line A measure down depth of bodice (point H).
8. From H draw a line across measuring half the width of the bodice. From the end of this line draw a vertical line the length of the underarm measurement; mark end I.
9. To make the armhole, join G and I in a shallow curved line
10. Draw a slightly curved line from F to E to mark neckline.
11. Dot a 15 mm seam allowance around the neck, shoulder, armhole, underarm and bottom of bodice.
12. Front and back bodices are the same, so write on pattern *Front/Back, Cut 2*.
13. Draw a vertical line to mark lengthwise grainline.

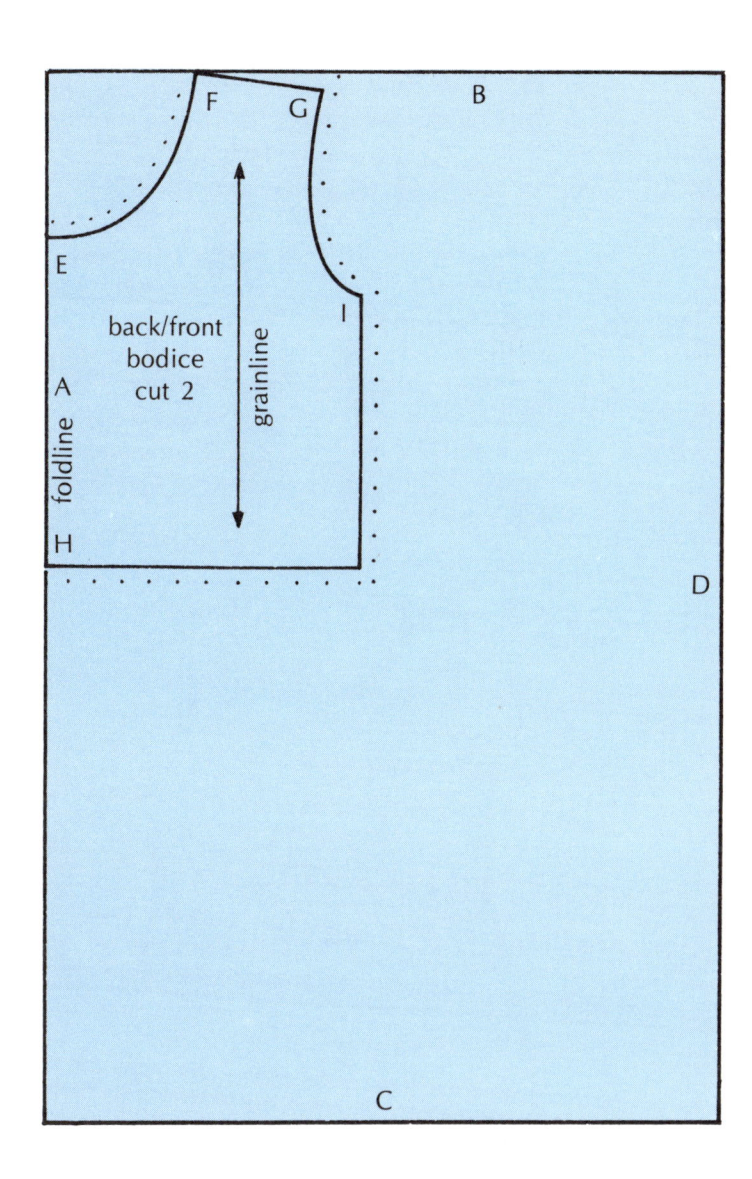

Skirt

1. On the left-hand side of the paper draw the length of the skirt plus hem allowance (mark this A).
2. From the top of line A and from the bottom, draw lines measuring half the width of the skirt plus gathering width (mark B and C).
3. Join the ends of B and C (mark this line D).
4. Write *Foldline* on line A.
5. Front and back skirts are the same—write on pattern *Front/Back, Cut 2*.
6. Draw a vertical line to mark lengthwise grainline.

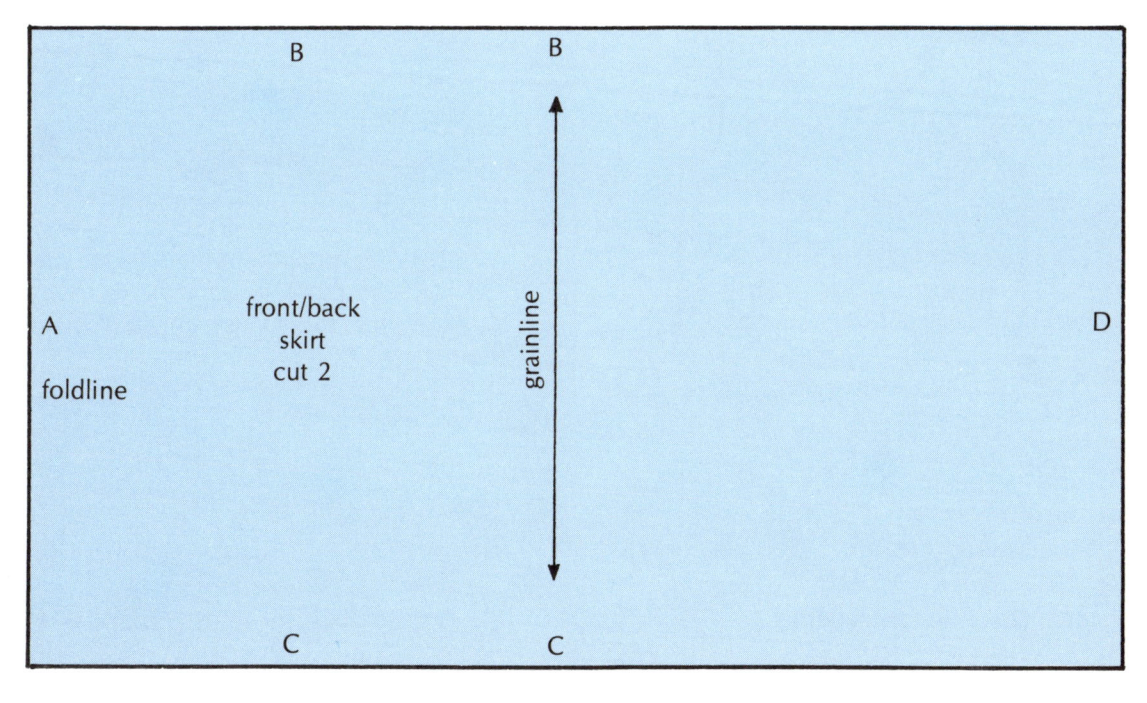

Making up

1. Pin and tack shoulder seams of front and back bodices together, machine and remove tacking. Press seams together towards back. Overlock or zig-zag the seams.
2. Sew a narrow hem at the edge of the neckline, neaten with an overlock stitch. Be careful not to stretch neckline. 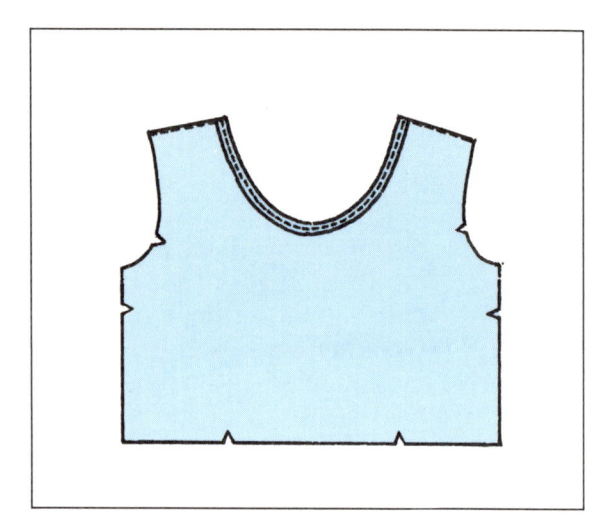
3. Sew around the armholes with the same method.
4. With right sides facing together, join side seams and neaten edges. Press seams towards the back. 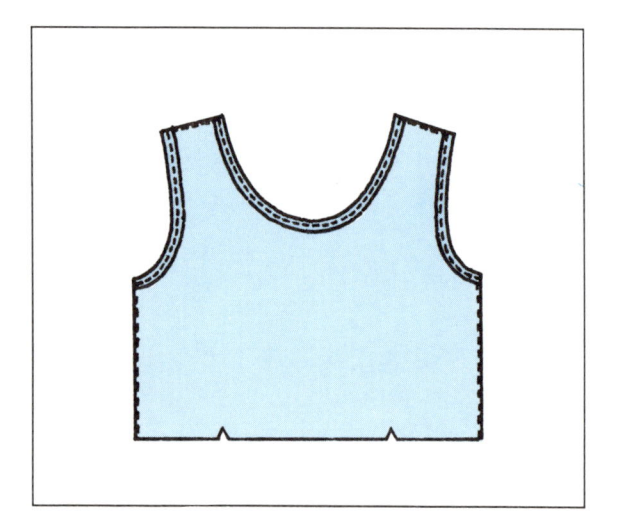
5. With right sides of skirt facing together, pin, tack and machine side seams; neaten seams. Press towards back.
6. Turn skirt to right side. Sew a gathering stitch 13 mm from top edge. Pull up the gathering thread to fit bodice.
7. With right sides of bodice and skirt together, pin centre of bodice to centre of skirt, match side seams, then evenly distribute gathers all the way around. Place pins vertically in between folds.
8. Tack and machine. Remove tacking, neaten raw edge and press seam up towards the top. 
9. Press 25 mm hem in place on skirt, machine close to edge of hem.
10. Hand-sew motif in the centre of the bodice.

Party frock (illustrated on page 39)

A fun and pretty frock for special occasions. The basic shape is a simple A line decorated with deep frills edged with satin ribbon. The sewing of the garment is all straight machining.

Materials required:

- If possible, choose a fabric wider than 90 cm to reduce the number of joins in the frills.

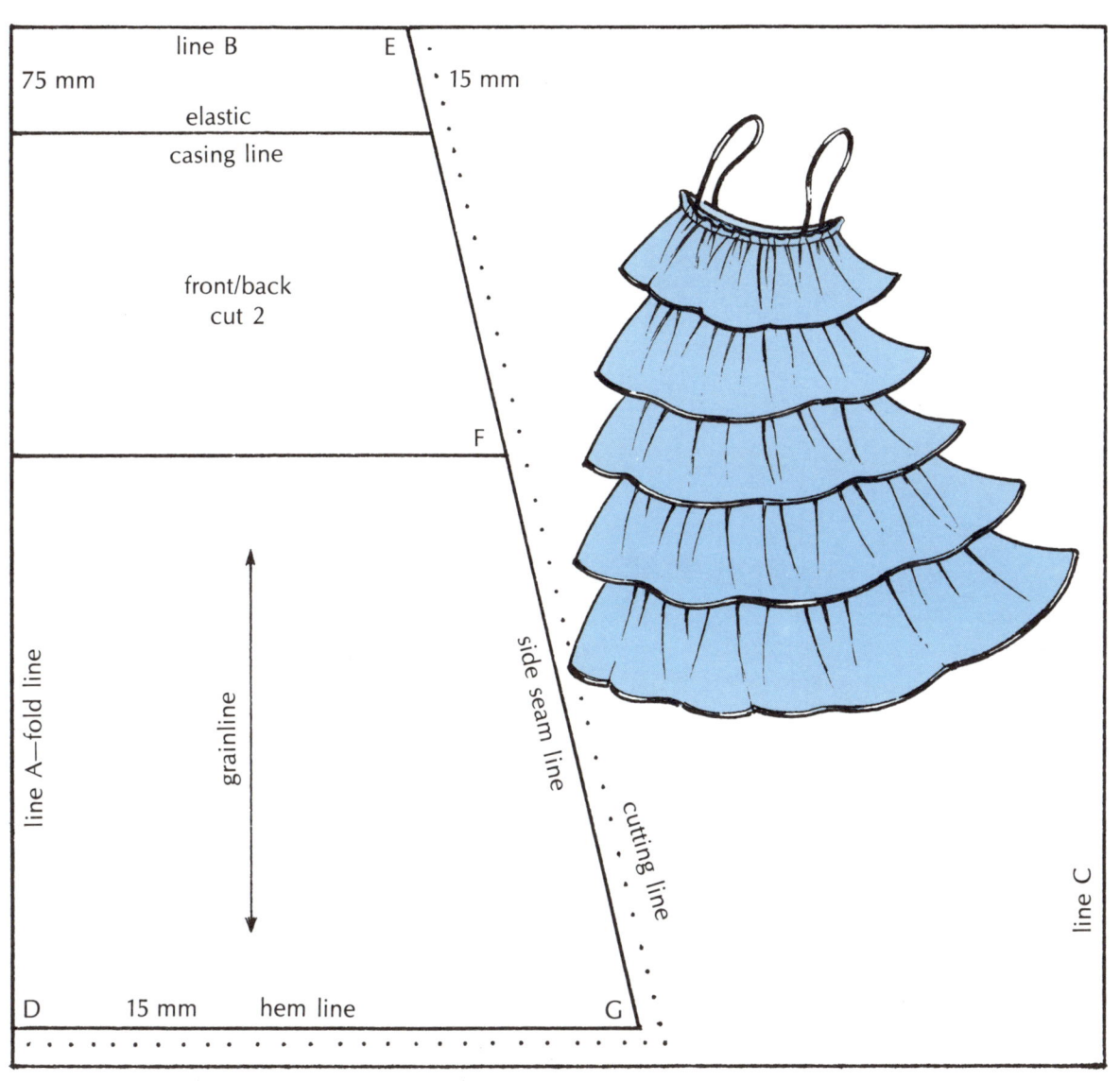

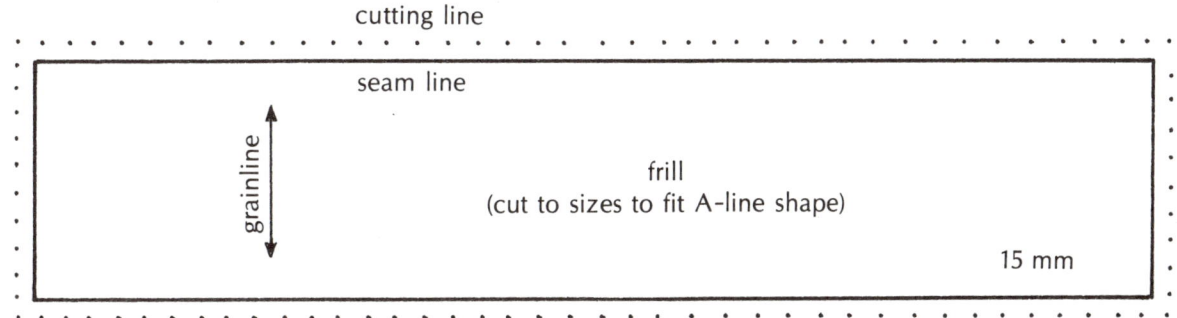

line B — E
75 mm
15 mm
elastic
casing line
front/back
cut 2
F
line A—fold line
grainline
side seam line
cutting line
line C
D   15 mm   hem line   G

cutting line

seam line
grainline
frill
(cut to sizes to fit A-line shape)
15 mm

Draft the basic pattern before you buy the material. Fullness of the frills is usually calculated by measuring around the garment at the frill position and adding half that measurement again.
- Matching colour thread
- Non-roll elastic 13 mm wide
- Ribbon to edge frills after sewing them to the garment; also allow for shoulder straps

Measurements:

1. Run a tape measure under the arms around the chest; add half this measurement again for threading elastic
2. Measure from underarm down to hem
3. Measure from underarm down to hipline
4. Measure hip, and add half the measurement again
5. Measure the length of the shoulder straps.

Drafting pattern

Use drafting paper 84 cm square.

1. Mark the left hand side of the drafting paper Line A and write *Fold line*.
2. Mark the top of the paper Line B.
3. Mark the right hand side of the paper Line C.
4. Measure from the top of line A the length from underarm to hem plus 75 mm to allow for elastic casing. Mark this point D, and draw the hemline right across the paper from D.
5. Measure from left-hand side of paper along Line B three-quarters of the chest measurement; mark this point E.
6. Measure from the top of line A the length from underarm to hipline. From this point draw a line across the paper measuring three-quarters of the hip measurement. Mark the end of this line F.
7. Draw a line joining points E and F. Extend it to meet the hemline, calling the intersection of the lines point G. This line becomes the side seamline. Add 15 mm seam allowance down side seamline and under hemline. Show this as a broken line (cutting line).
8. Measure 75 mm down line A and draw a line across the paper to meet the side seamline. This line is for the elastic casing.
9. Write *Front/Back, Cut 2* on the pattern, and draw a vertical line to mark lengthwise grainline.
10. Cut out pattern on cutting line.

Frills

Measure the length from the bottom of the casing to the hem and divide by the number of frills you want—probably 6, maybe 5 or 7. Add 15 mm seam allowance to the frill measurement. The bottom of the last frill should just meet the hemline.

Machining

1. With right sides of back and front together, pin, tack and machine side seams. Remove tacking. Press both seams towards the back, neaten edges with zig-zag stitch.
2. At top of garment, press seamline over on wrong side of garment and measure 75 mm down for elastic casing. Pin in place, machine along fold line, leaving a 25 mm opening for elastic.
3. Press up hem allowance on skirt, pin and machine close to edge.

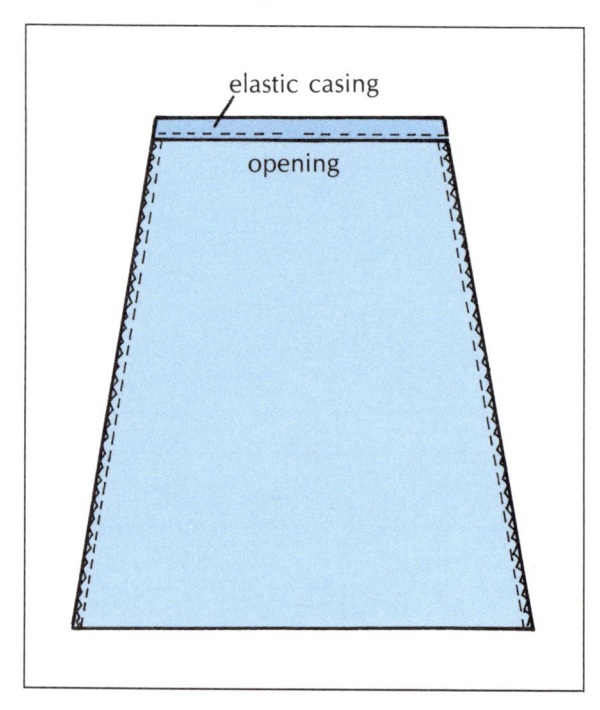

4. The A-line is now ready to have the first frill sewn at the top.
5. Join seams of frills, press flat. Press a tiny fold at the top of the frill, machine close to the edge to prevent fraying.
6. Machine a gathering stitch 15 mm from the top. 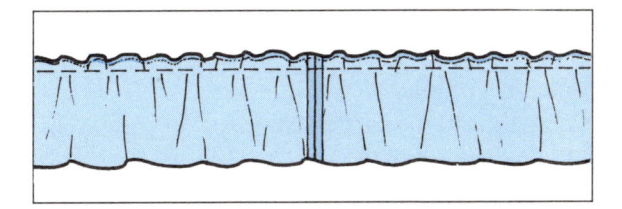
7. Place a piece of cardboard on the top of the ironing board. Lay the frock right side up over the cardboard.
8. With a pin mark the centre of the skirt, front and back, and the centre of the frill. Pin together and at side seams. Draw up gathering thread evenly between pinned area. Place pins vertically between folds.
9. Tack in place, machine all around and remove tacking. 
10. Pin and machine all the frills.
11. On edge of each frill press a tiny fold towards right side of material.
12. Pin satin ribbon to frill along fold line, encasing the raw edge of the fabric to prevent fraying. Start from the side seam each time.
13. Tack in the middle of the ribbon and machine each side close to the edge. Remove tacking. Press edge of frills with warm iron.
14. Thread elastic through casing to a comfortable fit. Hand-stitch lap of elastic. Machine across opening.
15. Mark positions for shoulder straps, fold raw edge of ribbon under and hand-sew in place.

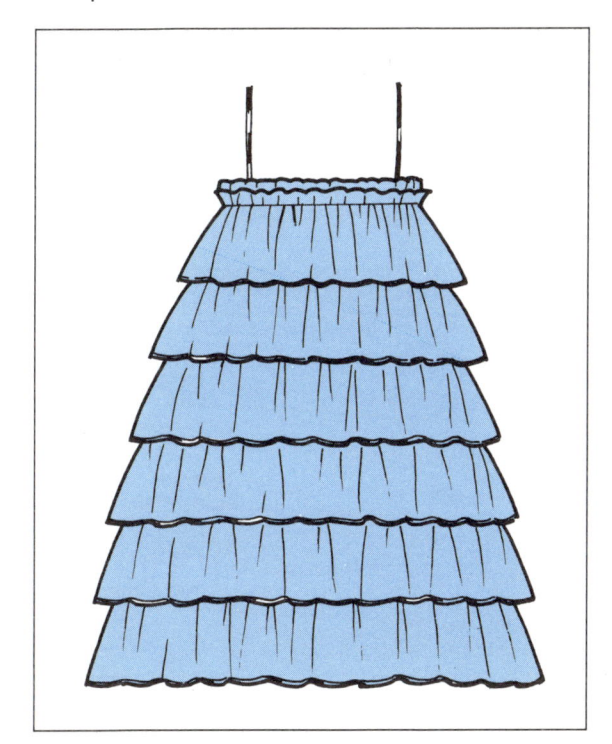

Board shorts *(illustrated on page 40)*

One sure way of making something you will like is to unpick an old, favourite pair of board shorts—in effect, a toile (page 15).

If you can't sacrifice some old shorts, buy a simple commercial pattern.

Materials required:

Buy fabric to measure twice the length of your shorts, plus seam allowances and hems.
Matching thread
Elastic (95 mm) or cord to go around your waist (allow for a tie with the cord).

1. Press the unpicked shorts and write *front* and *back* on each section. The back has a larger curve than the front for sitting and movement.
2. Press the fabric and mark the right side with a pin.
3. Fold the fabric with the right sides together (and the grainline running lengthwise), folding an area wide enough for the width of the shorts.
4. Pin front and back sections close to fold line and just below one another. Chalk around the pattern pieces. Leave a little extra for seam allowances if the original seams have frayed.
5. Cut out on chalk line and through fold line.
6. With right sides facing, pin the two back sections together down the centre back, tack and machine. A second line of stitching will make the seam stronger.

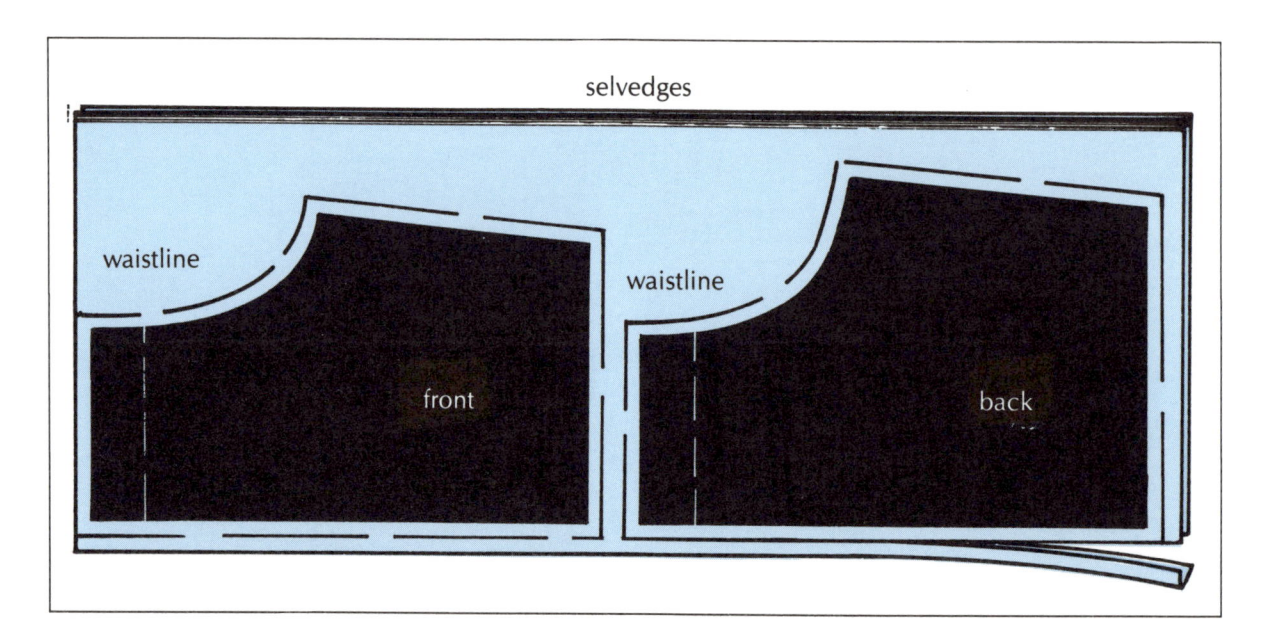

7. Trim the seam to about 7 mm, and zig-zag the raw edges together and press flat.
8. Repeat with front sections.
9. With right sides together, pin the front to the back down the inside and outside legs. Tack and machine zig-zag the raw edges together. Press seams towards the back.
10. Fold the top down 25 mm to the inside to make a waistband. Pin in place, leaving a 25 mm opening in the centre of the front to thread elastic or cord through.
11. Machine close to the edge.
12. Using a large safety-pin, thread elastic or cord through the waistband for a comfortable fit.
13. Fold up the hemline of the shorts, pin and tack, then machine. Press the completed garment.

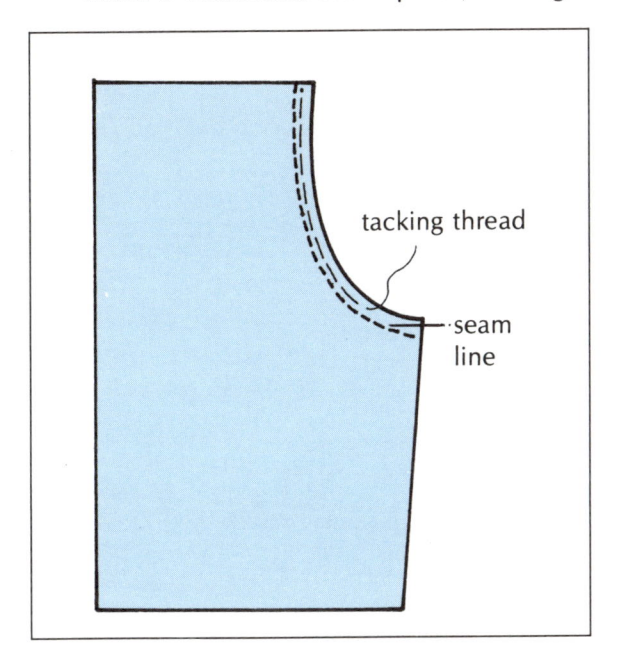

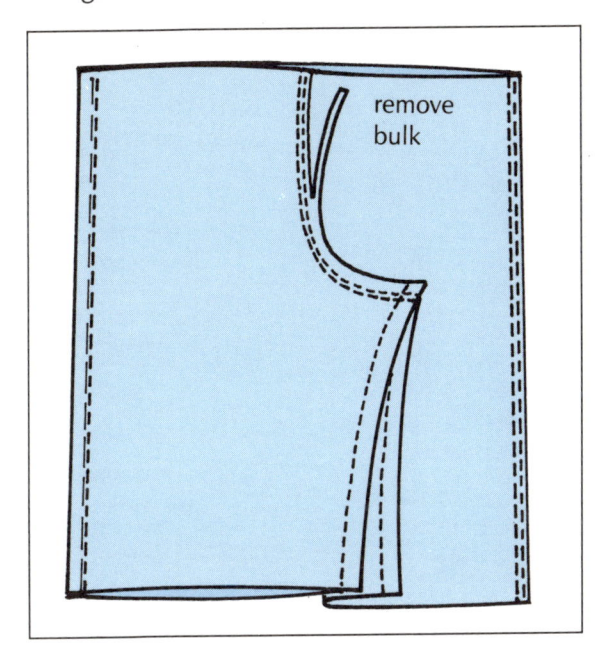

Index

accessories, 8
armhole, 45, 46

babywear, 19
basting, 17
bias, 13
bias strips, 26
bindings, 27, 32
   double, 27
blanket-stitch, 44
blazers, 53
blouse, 41
board shorts, 68
bodice darts, 24
box pleats, 50
buttonhole, 32, 49, 53
buttonhole position, 14
buttonhole stitch, 52
buttonholes, 9, 14, 52
buttons, 9, 49, 53
   sew-through, 53
   shank, 53

canvas, 2
chamois, 12
chart
   needle and thread, 12
children's clothes, 19
clothes
   children's, 19
   men's, 52, 53
   women's, 52, 53
collars, 30
   Peter Pan, 23, 30
   pointed, 23, 30
   shirt, 31
contour darts, 25
corduroy, 12
cotton, 8
cotton-covered polyester, 12
cottons, 16
crafts, 28
cuffs, 29, 32
cutting line, 14
cutting out, 16
cutting layout shading key, 16

dart line, 17
dart placements, 14
darts, 15, 24, 47
   bodice, 24
   contour, 25
   French, 24
   line, 17
   placement, 14
denim, 12
double binding, 27

evening gowns, 28

fabric, 9, 17, 21
fabrics, 18
   canvas, 12
   chamois, 12
   corduroy, 12
   cotton, 8
   denim, 12
   felt, 12
   garbardine, 12
   georgette, 12
   handkerchief linen, 12
   lace, 12
   lawn, 12
   leather, 12
   linen, 12
   organza, 12
   paper taffeta, 12
   polyester, 12
   poplin, 12
   sailcloth, 12
   shantung, 12
   silk, 9
   suedes, 12
   velour, 12
   velvet, 9, 12
   wool, 9, 19
facings, 20
felt, 12
fitting, 16
flannel, 12
foldline, 14
French darts, 24
French seams, 9, 19
frills, 29

garbardine, 12
gathered skirt, 56
gathering, 29
georgette, 12
gowns, 28
   evening, 28
   wedding, 28, 53
grain, 26
grainline, 13, 16, 21, 49

hand-sewing, 51
hand-sewn overcast seam, 18
handkerchief linen, 12
hem, 48
hemstitching, 51
Hong Kong seam, 19
hooks and eyes, 54

interfacing, 21
inverted pleats, 50

iron, 16
ironing, 9, 16, 18, 24
ironing board, 8

jackets, 23
jeans, 19

knife pleats, 50
knife-pleated skirt, 22
knits, 12

lace, 12
lawn, 12
leather, 12
Liberty print border and sash, 56
linen, 12
lingerie, 12

measurements, 10
men's clothes, 52, 53
millinery, 28

Needle and Thread Chart, 12
needles, 8, 18

organza, 12
overlapping edges, 54

paper taffeta, 12
party frock, 65
patch pockets, 48
patterns, 13
   board shorts, 68
   gathered skirt, 56
   party frock, 65
   pinafore, 62
   pleated skirt, 59
Peter Pan collar, 23, 30
pinafore, 62
placket, 32
pleat position, 15
pleated skirt, 59
pleats, 50
   box, 51
   inverted, 50
   knife, 50
   position, 15
pockets, 48
pointed collar, 23, 30
polyester, 12
poplin, 12
pressing, 9

raglan sleeve, 46
rouleaus, 28
run and fell seam (flat-felled), 19

sailcloth, 12
scissors, 8
seam line, 14, 15
seam, 9, 18, 20
  French, 9, 19
  hand-sewn overcast, 18
  Hong Kong, 19
  run and felled, 19
  flat-felled, 19
  stitched and turned, 18
  underarm, 45
  zigzagged, 18
selvedge, 13, 26
set-in sleeve, 45
sew-through buttons, 53
sewing machine, 8, 9
shank buttons, 53
shantung, 12
shirt collar, 31
shirt sleeve, 46
shoulder straps, 28
silk, 9
skirt, 42, 50

gathered, 56
knife-pleated, 22
pleated, 59
sleeves, 45
  raglan, 46
  set-in, 45
  shirt, 46
slipstitching, 51
sportswear, 19
stitched and turned seam, 18
stitch
  blanket, 44
  buttonhole, 52
  hem, 51
  top, 22, 23
  slip, 51
  under, 21
suedes, 12

tacking, 16, 17
tailor tacks, 14, 17
threads, 24
ticking, 12

toile, 15
topstitching, 22, 23

underarm seam, 45
understitching, 21

velours, 12
velvet, 9, 12

waistbands, 21, 41
waistcoats, 53
waistline, 50
waistlines, 29
warp, 13
wedding gowns, 28, 53
weft, 13
women's clothes, 52, 53
wool, 9, 19

zigzagged seam, 18
zips, 14, 42